The Real Guide To Teenage Depression

Handling Teen Depression A Book About What Matters Most For Teen Boys And Teen Girls.

PATRICE M FOSTER

© Copyright 2017 by Patrice M Foster - All rights reserved

The Real Guide to Teenage Depression

ISBN: 9780998187402

Library of Congress Control Number: 2016917551

This document is geared towards providing exact and reliable information in regards to the topic and issue covered. The publication is sold with the idea that the publisher is not required to render accounting, officially permitted, or otherwise, qualified services. If advice is necessary, legal or professional, a practiced individual in the profession should be ordered. From a Declaration of Principles which was accepted and approved equally by a Committee of the American Bar Association and a Committee of Publishers and Associations. In no way is it legal to reproduce, duplicate, or transmit any part of this document in either electronic means or in printed format. Recording of this publication is strictly prohibited and any storage of this document is not allowed unless with written permission from the publisher. All rights reserved.

Table of Content

Introduction — 1
   For Parents, Teachers, or Caregivers — 2
   For Teens — 4
   Disclaimer — 7

Chapter One: What Is Teenage Depression? — 8
   What is Depression? — 9
   Causes of Depression in the Teenage Years — 13
   Signs and Symptoms of Depression — 19
   Effects of Depression on Teens — 23
   In Summary — 26

Chapter Two: Types of Teenage Depression — 28
   Major Depression — 28
   Dysthymia — 30
   Bipolar Disorder — 33
   Seasonal Affective Disorder — 36
   Atypical Depression — 38
   Premenstrual Dysphoric Disorder — 40
   Psychotic Depression — 42
   Substance-Induced Mood Disorder — 45
   Postpartum Depression — 46
   In Summary — 49

Chapter Three: Bullying is More Than Just Words — 51

What Are Bullying and Cyberbullying?	52
The Connection Between Bullying and Suicide	56
Suicide Warning Signs	59
Why Suicide?	62
Shocking Statistics on Bullying and Cyberbullying	63
In Summary	66
Chapter Four: The Numbers Behind Teenage Depression	**68**
Get to Know the Numbers	69
Important Facts about Teenage Depression	74
How to Talk to Your Teen about Depression and Suicide	76
In Summary	80
Chapter 5: Depression and the Idiosyncratic Teen	**82**
Depression in Teens with Disabilities	84
Depression in Teens with Other Mental Disorders	87
Depression in Minority Teens	90
Depression in LGBTQIA Teens	92
In Summary	95
Chapter 6: Prevention and Treatment of Teen Depression	**97**
Ways Parents Can Prevent Depression	98
Ways Educators Can Prevent Depression	104
Ways Teens Can Prevent Depression	110
Treatment Options Available for Teens	121
Seeking Support for Yourself	125
Hotlines and Treatment Organizations	127

In Summary	131
Conclusion	**134**
Resources	**137**
Other Books by Patrice M Foster	**152**
Thank You	**153**

Introduction

Have you ever felt more than just a little down? Maybe at some point in your life, the future looked bleak or uninspiring. You felt as though there was no way anything could possibly look up again. Or maybe you didn't feel much of anything; maybe you simply dragged yourself out of bed every day, weary of feeling no excitement or interest in your life.

It could be that you've experienced more significant feelings of sadness. You could have felt an urge to physically or emotionally punish yourself through bodily harm or by forcing yourself to listen to negative self-talk. In any of these cases, you were likely experiencing the symptoms of depression.

No matter how old you are, depression is one of the most common mental illnesses there is. Think of depression like the common cold, and you'll have some idea of just how often those around you suffer from bouts of what is far more than just "the blues." Depression affects children, teens, and adults alike. However, during the teen years, when major life changes are already creating tension, recognizing and dealing with depression can be even more challenging.

Patrice M Foster

For Parents, Teachers, or Caregivers

For parents, teachers, and other adults who care for teens, learning to recognize the signs of depression in adolescents is an incredibly important part of raising healthy people. It can be hard to sort out what behavior is due to hormones or changing responsibilities and interests and what is truly due to depression. It could be both and in many cases, it will be.

In addition to recognizing the signs of depression, adults also need to be aware of the types of depression. For example, there are some types of depression that cause swings between manically happy or energetic behavior and completely uninterested, dejected behavior. There is depression that only strikes during certain parts of the year and depression that is directly related to outside factors like bullying. All of these different types can manifest in unique ways.

Another important point for parents learning about teen depression is to realize that teens don't act depressed to gain attention. Real depression cannot be faked, and healthy teens do not display the symptoms of depression on purpose. If a teen who is not depressed is displaying these symptoms, there

The Real Guide to teenage Depression

is another issue or illness at work that needs to be addressed just as the depression would need to be.

Parents often think back when their child was younger and happy and assume that there's just no way their teen can be depressed. They remember the days when their child laughed for hours at their own jokes or cheerfully jumped back up after getting hurt, insisting that they were fine. But the truth is that depression isn't based on a person's natural disposition.

A quiet, shy, introspective child may never face depression at all. This child may grow into a perfectly happy, healthy adult who also happens to be quiet and introspective. A bubbly, excitable child could face a lifelong struggle with depression. They'll still be their naturally optimistic self on the outside, but they'll also be struggling with a mental disorder that needs to be addressed. Remember, depression is just like the common cold: anyone can get it, and it doesn't reflect on the kind of person they are.

For parents and other adult caregivers, this book will help you understand how depression affects your teen and how you can help. Here's what we'll discuss:

- What depression is and what causes it.

- The types of depression and the different ways that each can manifest.
- The relationship between depression, bullying, and suicide and how you can help your child battle this ongoing issue throughout their toughest school years.
- The statistics surrounding teenage depression, as well as teenage suicide, self-harm, eating disorders, and many other outward symptoms of depression.
- How depression can affect teens with disabilities, disorders, or identities that fall outside of society's currently defined "norm."
- How to prevent or treat depression in teens.

Through these chapters, I hope to offer you the tools you need to give your teens a healthy, happy experience before becoming successful adults.

For Teens

Have you ever seen any of your friends or schoolmates change from one school year to the next? Maybe there used to be a nice, smart girl in the front row of every class who loved horses and books; but by the next year, she was sleeping through class

The Real Guide to teenage Depression

in the back, sitting alone during lunch, and covering her old horse folders with Sharpie scribbles.

Or maybe you've known friends who have started hurting themselves and covering the scars with long sleeves in the summer. Maybe you've heard a classmate forcing themselves to throw up after lunch, or you've noticed that a previously quiet boy is constantly getting into fights. Maybe some or all of these scenarios describes you.

In any of these cases, you or your classmates could be suffering from depression. Depression may sound like something that only stressed-out adults get, but it is nothing more than a sickness that needs medical attention. Like catching a cold or breaking a bone, it can happen to anyone.

Depression is also one of the least-understood illnesses, especially in teenagers. When you're already dealing with a heavier school schedule, undergoing the stress of choosing a college or a career, experiencing changes in your body, and many other things, it's hard to know what is just "normal hormone stuff" and what could be depression.

If you've ever had a prolonged period of feeling something is simply not right, however, it's likely this isn't normal. And you shouldn't have to worry that your parents or doctor will think you're just trying to get attention. Treating depression is very easy once the symptoms have been discussed head-on.

In this book, you can learn all you need to know to tackle depression in a logical and matter-of-fact way. You'll get information on what causes depression and what depression even is in the first place. You'll also find out about the different types of depression, so you'll know what to expect when you see a doctor. Statistics on teen depression can help you talk to your parents or your doctor, and we'll also discuss how bullying and difficult peer relationships can make depression worse.

In Chapter Five, we'll specifically discuss teens who have disabilities or disorders or who identify in ways that fall outside of society's norm. Teens who are LGBTQIA, neuro-atypical, or face other challenges can be affected by depression in very different ways.

Finally, we'll discuss ways to prevent yourself from developing depression and how doctors or counselors may treat depression if you are experiencing it. These are important things to remember:

- Anyone can suffer from depression no matter their age, lifestyle, or personality.
- If you feel depressed, you aren't "just trying to get attention," and it's important that you seek help.
- Depression is treatable, and you don't have to feel this way forever.

Disclaimer

Nothing in this book is intended to replace medical advice. If you believe you are experiencing depression or you believe that a teen you know or care for is depressed, you should always seek the attention of a trained medical professional.

Knowing when to seek out a doctor and what to expect if and when you do can make it much easier to tackle depression and get back to a happy and healthy life. If you're ready to learn more and to empower yourself and the teens around you, read on.

Patrice M Foster

Chapter One: What Is Teenage Depression?

When it comes to understanding teenage depression, Hollywood is working against us. How many movies or TV shows have you seen where the moody or Gothic teen is played for laughs? The surly teenage son or daughter is just one more annoyance that the goofy parents have to deal with, and so often their insistence that they wear all black or that they don't smile in the family portrait is solved after a few laugh tracks.

The problem with this picture is that it makes teenage depression seem like something that can be turned off with the right amount of persuading. The teenager in question is nothing more than an attention hog, demanding that everyone acknowledge how "sad" they are—until Mom slips the teen extra allowance to wear a pretty dress. Then the depression is suddenly, magically gone.

Real depression is nothing like this, and the fact that we see this message so often creates an intensely dangerous environment for teens who do experience depression. Understanding what depression is and what causes it is the first step to helping teens face and overcome depression.

Depression is a mental condition that affects many teens throughout the world, and it is becoming much more common and problematic. On the outside, the condition will appear to cause teens sadness that does not go away with time. They may begin to lose interest in their favorite activities or withdraw from the outside world. When depression is not recognized, is pushed to the side, or is denied, other problems may arise including drug abuse, self-harm, or worse.

What is Depression?

On a scientific level, this is the definition of depression:

"Depression is a mood disorder that causes a persistent feeling of sadness and loss of interest. Also called major depressive disorder or clinical depression, it affects how you feel, think, and behave and can lead to a variety of emotional and physical problems."

This definition from the Mayo Clinic best sums up the general explanation of depression. It's a disorder that affects the mood and can eventually affect the body as well. But what causes this disorder? With illnesses, a bacteria or virus is sometimes to blame. Is there something like this that causes depression?

As it turns out, medical scientists believe that depression is a combination of both a medical issue within the brain, as well as a natural emotional response to certain stimuli. As a medical disease, a chemical imbalance in the brain is often blamed for depression.

There are specific chemicals in the brain, particularly serotonin and norepinephrine, that help the human body regulate a consistently peaceful mood. Although some doctors say that a reduction in the neurotransmitters that carry these chemicals can cause depression, others say that the lack of these chemicals in the brain is a symptom of depression, not a cause.

This "chicken or egg" problem hasn't been fully cleared up. Another popular medical opinion thought to explain depression is that the brain can overproduce stress hormones. This can cause a variety of negative symptoms in the brain:

- A lack of appetite.
- A higher sense of danger and alertness.

The Real Guide to teenage Depression

- A shutdown of brain activities that aren't deemed essential such as short-term memory. This explains why depressed teens may find it incredibly difficult to maintain good grades.
- More energy being delivered to the muscles, which can cause feelings of restlessness or a need to engage in extreme physical activity.

Basically, when the brain is filled with stress hormones, it enters a state in which it is preparing to fight. The body and mind feel as though they are under threat and begin acting accordingly. The truth is that they are under threat—it's just that the threat is coming from within.

But these medical causes still don't quite explain what causes depression. The other side of the coin is the psychology of depression. Doctors state that in addition to higher stress hormones and lower brain chemical production, the way we react emotionally to the world around us can be a major cause of depression.

For example, did you know that people are now ten times more likely to develop depression than those born before 1945? Life is very different now than it was in 1945. One large change includes the higher rate of divorce compared to marriage in earlier decades. A teen from seventy years ago would not have had to deal with the same kind of extreme mental and emotional stress that comes with living through a divorce.

This is only one example of how our changing society has created situations in which teens can frequently face high-stress stimuli that their brains are not able to deal with in a healthy manner. From the overwhelming presence of media and news to the higher focus on material success, teens face more stressors by the day.

So what is the answer? What causes depression? Overall, some or all of these factors can combine to cause depression:

- Imbalanced brain chemicals.
- Increased stress hormones.
- Unhealthy emotional responses to increased stressful situations.
- A changing society that presents more overwhelming stimuli than ever before.

Any combination of these things can be responsible for the depression a teen faces.

Causes of Depression in the Teenage Years

Everything we discussed above is a good general description of what depression is and what causes it. But just as you might expect a fever to affect an infant differently from the way it affects an adult, depression and the teen years can be an entirely new beast. There are a few other causes specifically related to the growing teenage body that could be behind depression.

Teenage Hormones

As the teen body changes from child to adult, the hormone production in the brain starts kicking into overdrive. All hormones, from the sexual hormones to the growth hormones, are stepping up to help the body move to a new phase. If you'll remember from earlier, an increase in the stress hormone can be a very negative thing.

What happens when the brain, merrily pumping out the same hormones that are causing acne and awkward body hair, doesn't quite differentiate between one hormone and the next?

If the stress hormone begins to flood the teenage body, depression can quickly follow.

In fact, one of the most common causes of depression in teens is hormonal changes. Typically, teenage girls are more likely to experience depression due to the rapid rate of change in the female body. A study conducted by the [Substance Abuse and Mental Health Services Administration](#) says that girls between the ages of twelve and fifteen are three times more likely to experience depression than boys of the same age.

Childhood Trauma

It's a well-observed phenomenon that children who suffered from any sort of trauma during younger years will often not experience the profound mental and emotional aftershocks until the teen years. "Trauma" can be anything from abuse to a car accident or the death of a close loved one.

But as teens become older and better understand the truth of what happened and the way the trauma will or has shaped their lives, it's common for them to experience a season of depression. In this case, the depression could be caused in large part by an unhealthy reaction to an overwhelming understanding of a past experience.

When teens have gone through a serious life event, it is vital that they receive the care and support they need to help them cope with their feelings. In addition to treating the depression with medication or therapy, affected teens will also need to receive therapy or other treatment for the trauma itself. Support groups and other such treatments will be vital to healing both the depression and the lingering effects of the trauma.

Hereditary Imbalances

Did you know that if you as a parent have experienced depression, your teen could be up to 50 percent more likely to experience depression? [A study](#) by Stanford School of Medicine showed that those who have siblings with major depression could be as much as two or three times more likely than average to experience depression as well. While the existence of a "depression gene" hasn't been proven, there is no way to deny that being around someone who is depressed can affect a teen.

If the depression is directly linked to a chemical imbalance in the brain or an overproduction of stress hormones, then it's very likely there is something in the DNA that is causing people in your family to experience depression. But if the depression was caused more by a reaction to a situation or certain stimuli, consider the possibility that something you experienced also affected your teen. That means your teen went through the same situation or experienced the same stimuli you did "secondhand." You could have been facing depression due to a bad working environment; but whether you realized it or not, you brought that stress home with you, and that could cause a teen to experience the same negative feelings.

Another Illness

There are several reasons why being diagnosed with another illness could cause teens to suffer from depression. If the original illness includes chronic or severe pain or limits the teen from participating in regular activities, it's easy to see how they could become depressed very quickly.

Medication prescribed for an unrelated illness is another factor to look out for. Certain medications are known to cause depression:

- If a teen girl is on birth control, the risk of depression is much higher. This is because birth control is a hormone-altering drug. Transgender teens who take hormone therapy could also be affected by their medication.
- Stimulants like Ritalin and Adderall, which are often prescribed for ADHD, have been known to cause depression. These medications increase the level of certain chemicals in the brain, which can lead to an imbalance.
- Medicines that are used to prevent seizures affect the neurotransmitters in the brain, which can block or change the way chemicals are transferred to different parts of the brain.
- Medications that are meant to treat irritable bowel syndrome or other GI disorders can cause depression because they act as a depressant for the central nervous system.
- Muscle relaxers or other benzodiazepine hypnotics, which are often prescribed for sleeping disorders or anxiety, can cause depression. These medications act as a depressant for the central nervous system in order to treat the original illness.

- Corticosteroids used to treat lupus, arthritis, and other illnesses can cause depression due to their tendency to lower the serotonin levels in the brain.
- You may not think that beta-blockers, typically used to treat high blood pressure, would be prescribed to teens; but these medications can also be used to treat migraines, heart murmurs, and tremors. These medications can cause fatigue and depression, though it is unclear exactly why.

Additionally, antidepressants meant to treat depression and anxiety have been known to worsen depression or to cause other dependency issues. If a teen has been diagnosed with another illness, particularly if they are taking a new medication, it's important to watch for any signs of depression.

Bullying and Other Social Problems

Later in this book, we'll go in-depth into bullying and how social problems can affect teens. But for now, it's important to note this very common cause of depression. When teens suffer from a social disorder or they are not socially accepted by their peers, they can begin to withdraw and become depressed, feeling alone and hopeless that life will ever be fulfilling. Bullying is a serious situation and when coupled with depression, it becomes that much more serious. Alarming studies show that social bullying and accompanying depression leads to self-harm and suicide more frequently than the average parent may realize.

These causes are the most common reasons why teens experience depression, but they are certainly not the only reasons. It is important to remember that there are many types of depression and every single case of depression will be unique because every teen is unique. Therefore, coping with depression and choosing the right treatment can take some time and trial.

Signs and Symptoms of Depression

Above, we listed many of the common causes of depression. In each of these cases it is important that you are able to recognize the symptoms of depression. If you find yourself feeling sad or you notice a teen who seems to be less cheerful or energetic than usual, it's easy to dismiss these signs as "just having a bad day," a lack of restful sleep, or stress over the many new decisions and responsibilities teens face.

But by dismissing these signs, it becomes that much easier for the depression to worsen and lead to serious consequences. Therefore, knowing the signs of depression and acting upon them when they are noticed is the best way to keep yourself or a teen healthy.

Remember again that all teens will experience depression differently. For instance, one teen may withdraw from social activities, while another may get involved in many new activities in an attempt to find excitement or interest in life again. It is not uncommon for teens to try to hide that they are depressed. Often, teens are conditioned to believe they will be punished or shamed for "seeking attention," so they may pretend to still partake in their daily routine to prevent a conversation about their feelings or to make sure no one recognizes there may be a problem.

Also, keep in mind that when teens are depressed, they may only show certain symptoms one day and not the next. The symptoms they display can change with their mood. These are some of the most common symptoms:

- Feelings of self-doubt or worthlessness.

- Feeling overwhelmed, frustrated, or disappointed with occurrences in daily life.
- Being unable to concentrate or memorize facts when studying.
- Feeling paralyzed by decisions.
- Failing to complete tasks like homework or chores that used to be easy.
- Thinking that the people in your life would be better off without you.
- Physical illness including stomachaches, muscle pain, headaches, and tiredness.
- Significant weight loss or gain.
- Decline or major shift in physical and social activities.
- Changes in any sleeping and eating patterns.
- Suicidal thoughts or self-harm activities.
- Crying and strong feelings of sadness.
- Anger and irritability.
- Loss of interest in favorite activities.
- Drug or alcohol abuse.

Experiencing only a few of these could be the result of other things. For example, teens may choose to change their social activities as their tastes and interests naturally change with age. But experiencing several at the same time or experiencing any of these to a serious extreme should be monitored. If the feeling or behavior persists, it is probably time to consider seeking a medical opinion and treatment.

For parents, teachers, or caregivers, it can be difficult to determine what is considered depression and what is considered just a bad day. One of the best things you can do is speak with the teen about the symptoms you've observed. Of course, not all teens are going to open up. Privacy during the teen years is an important right, and adults may find themselves being left out of the loop as teens try to understand their bodies and symptoms on their own at first.

If this happens, the best thing to do is to make yourself available, letting the teen know you are there to help or listen when they are ready to talk. If you are directly responsible for the health and well-being of the teen, pay attention to behavior and track it. Doing this can help you understand the difference between the teen's moods. Over time, it can become very apparent what is a bad day and what is an extended bout of depression.

If the teen will not open up to you and you've observed what you suspect is depression, then the next step may be to suggest that the teen speak to a doctor. By allowing them to seek out an impartial third party, they may be comfortable enough to discuss what they have been feeling without worrying that they are somehow letting you down or feeling guilty for seeking attention.

Effects of Depression on Teens

The signs and symptoms listed above can and do happen to teens who experience depression—but those are mostly the standard symptoms that anyone can experience when dealing with this illness. There are certain things that should be understood about the way depression can specifically affect the body and the vulnerable teenage brain.

The word "vulnerable" doesn't sound very comforting. But understanding how and why this word applies to adolescent brains can help make sense of some of the signs of depression. One of the first effects parents and teachers will probably notice right away is that a teen begins to do badly in school.

Whether your child was a straight "A" student before or walks a fine line between passing and failing, a large decline in grades and the quality of schoolwork or an increase in the number of classes they fail is very noticeable. Many times, teens could start skipping classes altogether as they struggle with their depression.

Another effect that depression can have on teens is in the form of substance abuse and violence. If they start to take an unhealthy interest in drugs, cigarettes, or alcohol, this can be a major warning sign for the adults around them. Some people rely on these substances to try to medicate themselves and provide an escape from the pain, but in actuality, they are making the problem worse as they form an addiction or accidentally overdose.

Violence is also concerning, especially when it reaches the point that teens are hurting other people or leaving holes in the walls. Irritability can be normal as teens learn to handle changing hormones, but when the violence or irritability becomes scary or concerning, there is a problem.

At-risk teens may also begin to express these thoughts:

- "I am just a worthless kid."
- "I can't live up to anyone's expectations."
- "I am ugly. No one will ever want me."

Low self-esteem can occur in any child, and when it suddenly comes on, adults should address the issue right away. Low self-esteem and feelings of self-doubt and worthlessness can lead to self-harm, which is dangerous and can be life threatening in many cases.

In all of these examples, there is a shared factor: it can be hard to differentiate between depression and the changes that the brain is going through during the teen years. The "problem" (which really isn't a problem, as you'll see) is that before the age of about twenty-five, the prefrontal cortex of the brain is still highly malleable.

This area of the brain is what allows us to understand our behavior, to make goals and plans, to make decisions, and to act appropriately in social situations. It is also what largely dictates a person's individual personality. As we reach full adulthood, the prefrontal cortex fully matures, which means that the chemicals responsible for the various things that the prefrontal cortex does have reached an optimal balance and our bodies have reached a state of harmony.

In the teenage brain, this hasn't happened yet. The prefrontal cortex is still learning to use and produce the right amounts of chemicals. And what's more, many studies have shown that the added stress from living in our society, from childhood trauma, and from teenage drug or alcohol abuse, as well as other causes of depression can actually change the way the prefrontal cortex will develop going forward.

This means that a teen experiencing depression is more likely to naturally develop a brain that is predisposed to depression. And this is why the teenage brain could be considered vulnerable.

In Summary

This chapter covered the explanation of depression, from both a scientific and a societal view. We learned that depression can be thought of as either a change in brain chemicals, a change in the production of hormones, an unhealthy response to outward stimuli, or a combination of any of the three.

We also discussed just a few of the many underlying causes of teen depression:

- Hormonal imbalances.

- Childhood trauma.
- Hereditary imbalances.
- Another illness.
- Bullying and other social problems.

We also discussed the many signs and symptoms that could accompany depression in teens, as well as the ways depression can specifically affect teenage brain development. Those who experience depression as teens are often more likely to experience depression as adults because of the way the brain is physically changed by the effects of depression.

Chapter One is an important place to highlight or bookmark in this book. Pay attention to the list of signs and symptoms of depression, and don't be afraid to start recording them if you notice them in yourself or in a teen you care for.

In the next chapter, we'll dive into the different types of depression and how each can manifest.

Chapter Two: Types of Teenage Depression

When it comes to teenage depression, no one type fits all. There are a number of different types of depression that occur, and what teens experience will depend on their situation and their symptoms. In addition, some teens may experience anxiety or other conditions coupled with their depression, making it harder to find the right diagnosis and treatment.

In Chapter Two, we'll look at nine types of teenage depression that are diagnosed and treated throughout the United States every year. Remember, this book is not meant to replace medical advice. While this information can help you better understand what to look for, it is not to be used for self-diagnosis. Always seek a medical professional to get a proper diagnosis.

Major Depression

Also called "Major Depressive Disorder," major depression occurs when teens experience a series of symptoms nearly daily for at least two weeks. At least one of the regular symptoms must be a loss of interest in activities or feelings of unrelenting sadness for a doctor to consider depression "major depression." The symptoms will continue much longer than the two weeks if the condition goes undiagnosed or unrecognized.

Teens who are experiencing a major episode of depression will often experience these symptoms:

- Irritability and anger.
- Lack of concentration in school.
- Poor performance in school.
- Feelings of worthlessness, guilt, and lowered self-esteem.
- Thoughts or talking of suicide.
- Sadness or crying.
- Increased sensitivity.
- Trouble sleeping and tiredness.
- Changes in the way they eat or the onset of an eating disorder.
- Substance abuse.
- Weight loss or gain.
- Feeling either "too slow" or "sped up."
- Loss of interest in activities.

- Inability to make decisions.

Teens who go through major depression are deeply saddened and without any type of treatment or relief from their feelings, they may begin to inflict harm on themselves. The type of harm teens can inflict on themselves will vary. This could include physical harm, an eating disorder, or emotionally harming themselves with negative self-talk.

For example, if teens are experiencing a lot of pain, they may cut themselves to express the pain in order to "punish" themselves for feeling weak or to help relieve some of the pain. Other teens may exhibit new, risky behaviors, including trying new drugs, new sexual experiences, and changing their friends.

Dysthymia

Dysthymia is a word that most people probably haven't heard; but when you are talking about teen depression specifically, it's an important one to know. Dysthymia, also called "chronic depression" or "persistent depressive disorder," often begins earlier in life, even in the childhood years.

The Real Guide to teenage Depression

As far as the severity of symptoms is measured, dysthymia is often thought of as a step down from major depression. A teen who is experiencing this type of depression will typically display two or more of the common depression symptoms to a lesser degree.

Where dysthymia differs from major depression is the length of time the symptoms have persisted. Rather than lasting for two weeks, chronic depression is defined by a prolonged period of depression, lasting for at least six months but often for several years at a time. The American Psychiatric Association (APA) defines dysthymia as depression lasting for at least two years.

Teens who experience dysthymia can often still function on a more normal level, and they often do not have trouble in their social lives or with grades unlike those with major depression. They may experience a few months of feeling completely normal, with no depressed feelings or symptoms at all, before relapsing into a depressed state.

As dysthymia fades in and out at a gradual pace, affected teens may come to believe that the depression symptoms are simply part of their personalities. Because the APA suggests that chronic depression is diagnosed after two years, it can be harder to get the right treatment right away. For these two reasons, dysthymia could actually be harder to handle than major depression.

While suicidal thoughts or self-harming behaviors aren't as common with dysthymia, there are still some unique symptoms to watch for:

- Low to no sexual drive during or after the onset of puberty.
- Having a variety of unexplainable physical symptoms that don't seem to be caused by an illness.
- Feeling irritable, guilty, hopeless, indecisive, or having low self-esteem on a regular, prolonged basis.
- Either insomnia or hypersomnia.
- The inability to regulate appetite on a normal basis, overeating, or undereating.
- Having very low energy on a regular basis.

Any of these symptoms lasting for at least six months could be signs that a teen is experiencing chronic depression. Recording symptoms and the length of time they have been present will be extremely important in getting the proper diagnosis.

Bipolar Disorder

You have probably heard of bipolar disorder, but you may not fully understand what it is. There are so many misconceptions about bipolar disorder that it is easy to confuse this condition with a personality disorder.

Bipolar disorder is also referred to as manic depression. It is a depressive illness just like dysthymia or major depression. In this condition, a teen's mood can change drastically between extreme levels of mania and depression. There will be periods of a level, "normal" mood in between, but the manic and depressive episodes will be so extreme, it will be impossible to categorize them as normal behavior.

The teen may be phenomenal one minute—absolutely on top of the world and filled with an obsessive energy that can't be contained—yet may feel horrible just hours or days later, as though there could never be anything in the world worth living for.

It can be difficult to recognize exactly what is going on, both as a teen experiencing bipolar disorder and as a person witnessing it. The manic behavior, which appears energetic and happy (if in a very extreme way), will often be accompanied by other symptoms of depression. The teen who seems maniacally energetic and excited will simultaneously experience fatigue, have trouble concentrating or making decisions, or will display other symptoms of depression.

To complicate matters further, there are several types of bipolar disorder:

- Bipolar I disorder is characterized by cycling between mania and depression. Each extreme lasts for at least seven days at a time. The episodes of mania could be so severe as to require hospitalization. The teen may pass out or harm themselves by accident, enter a psychotic state, or begin partaking in risky behaviors during these extreme mood swings.

- Bipolar II disorder is characterized by a milder state of mania, called hypomanic episodes. The mood swings between mania and depression will still be noticeable, but they are usually not severe enough to require hospitalization.

- Cyclothymic disorder is the term used to describe bipolar disorder that doesn't fall into either category. The teen may sometimes experience extreme manic episodes or their cycles between mania and depression may not take at least seven days as with Bipolar I.

In order to understand exactly what bipolar disorder looks like, you'll need to understand the signs of mania. The depressive mood swings will typically result in the same symptoms as classic depression. Manic episodes may include these signs and symptoms:

- Excessive, abnormal elation.
- Unusual irritability.
- Feeling totally rested after very little sleep.
- Increased sense of grandiose self-esteem.
- Constant talking or feeling pressured to constantly talk.
- Feeling as though your thoughts are racing.
- Indulging in an unhealthy or unsafe amount of pleasurable activities.
- An unusually noticeable increase in energy.
- A sudden decrease in judgment or "common sense.

- Inability to control behavior in social situations.
- Highly distractible and unable to concentrate.

If episodes that contain at least two or more of these symptoms are followed by cycles of depression and this pattern continues for several months, it is absolutely imperative that the teen see a doctor as soon as possible. Bipolar disorder often leads to putting oneself in danger, self-harm, or suicidal thoughts and actions.

Seasonal Affective Disorder

Seasonal depression, or seasonal affective disorder, is a type of depression that affects a person every year around the same time. It is almost always observed during the winter months, particularly in places where it gets dark and cold during the winter. However, there are rare cases of summer seasonal depression.

The exact cause of seasonal depression isn't known, but based on the science, we can make a pretty good guess. During the winter, when we are forced to stay inside more, we don't get as much sunlight. This causes the brain to make less serotonin, which in turn means that the brain can't regulate moods as easily.

This doesn't exactly explain everything, though. Summer seasonal depression can't be blamed on a lack of sunlight even for those who stay inside due to extreme heat. But the fact that seasonal depression is found overwhelmingly in areas where winters are dark and cold makes a good case for this explanation.

Seasonal affective disorder often begins in the teen and young adult years and is more likely to affect women than men. Most of the usual depression symptoms can be observed with seasonal depression. Weight gain and feeling a greater appetite are very common in winter seasonal depression while weight loss and a low appetite are common in summer seasonal depression.

One interesting way that seasonal depression differs from other types of depression is the way it is treated. Although other types of depression typically rely on combinations of medication, therapy, and lifestyle changes, many people have found relief from seasonal depression simply by getting more vitamin D or by using a solar lamp that mimics the natural light of the sun for a few hours a day. "Light therapy" tricks the brain into producing more serotonin, thus eliminating the assumed cause of seasonal depression.

Atypical Depression

The APA recently changed the classification of atypical depression to a subset of major depression; but however your doctor looks at it, atypical depression can be one of the most difficult forms of depression to understand and to diagnose. The best way to describe this type of depression is as major depression with mood improvement in positive situations.

One of the key symptoms of major depression is that even in a positive situation, surrounded by loved ones or when experiencing a great personal achievement, the teen still won't feel happy or interested. Atypical depression is depression that can be improved by these things, if only for the time spent in that situation. After leaving the positive situation, the depression will return.

Just as in major depression, atypical depression is diagnosed after at least two of the standard depression symptoms are experienced or observed almost daily for at least two weeks.

Teens who experience atypical depression may also resort to self-harm, destructive behaviors, or have thoughts or talk of suicide. Here are symptoms that are unique to atypical depression:

- A mood that temporarily lifts due to positive experiences.
- Significant weight gain and increase in appetite.
- Feeling as though the arms and legs are too heavy.
- Experiencing aches in the body.
- Extended periods of deep sleep.
- Unusually extreme negative responses to criticism or rejection.

In many cases, atypical depression is the result of some kind of trauma. A family going through a divorce, the death of a loved one, abuse, or a life-changing ordeal such as an accident can all bring about atypical depression. Substance abuse or being diagnosed with another illness are also thought to be some of the common causes of atypical depression.

Atypical depression can be hard to track when you are seeking a diagnosis for yourself or for a teen you care for. Your symptoms, recent life experiences, past experiences, family medical history, medications, or other factors can all play a part. Even if you feel as though your mood does improve from time to time, pay attention to the periods of depression that you (or a teen you care for) experience. Extreme persistent sadness that only goes away due to a happy situation is not normal.

Premenstrual Dysphoric Disorder

Premenstrual dysphoric disorder, or PMDD, is not simply "severe PMS." This is classified as a depressive disorder and can begin as soon as the teen starts having periods. The symptoms of PMDD are usually amplified during a teen girl's period, but the depression that accompanies the physical symptoms can last throughout the entire month.

About 5 percent of all women experience PMDD, and most of them begin experiencing it during their teen years. There are a number of symptoms of PMDD:

- Mood swings and irritability.
- Anxiety.
- Fatigue.
- Trouble staying focused.
- Extreme changes in appetite or sleeping patterns.

- Feeling extremely overwhelmed.
- Loss of interest in favorite activities.
- A persistent feeling of sadness or anger that can't be controlled.
- Physical symptoms such as body aches, headaches, bloating, and so on.

Although these look like typical PMS symptoms, PMDD sufferers will experience these symptoms, as well as symptoms of classic depression, to a much higher degree.

Premenstrual dysphoric disorder is usually diagnosed if the teen feels at least seven to ten days of well-being and stable health between periods. In most studies, PMDD is connected to fluctuating hormones in the teen's brain. Therefore, teen girls who take birth control, transgender teen boys who take testosterone hormones, or teens who are on hormone therapy for other medical conditions may find they are more susceptible to PMDD.

On the other hand, if a natural fluctuation in hormones is behind PMDD, birth control or other hormone therapy medicines may be prescribed to treat PMDD. Because PMDD is related to both depression, as well as the function of the menstrual cycle, there may be two treatments required: one for the depression and one for the effects on the menstrual cycle.

Unlike other types of depression, PMDD is usually diagnosed by a gynecologist rather than a psychiatrist or other type of medical doctor. At least two months of noticeable symptoms around the time of the period are usually required to diagnose PMDD.

Psychotic Depression

Psychotic depression is another subset of major depression, similar to atypical depression. The main difference between psychotic depression and major depression is that the symptoms of psychotic depression are also accompanied by forms of psychosis. These are just a few of the psychotic symptoms that can accompany the signs of classic depression in a teen:

- Hallucinations, including seeing, hearing, smelling, or otherwise sensing anything that isn't really there.
- Delusions, including feelings of intense guilt as though you have committed an unforgivable sin or have failed in a monumental way.

- Losing touch with reality.
- Having illogical thoughts, such as believing that another person can hear your thoughts or believing you are possessed.
- Extreme anger for no apparent reason.
- Confused speech or becoming selectively nonverbal.
- Becoming unable to physically move or suffering from intellectual impairment.
- Insomnia.
- A disregard for personal hygiene.

Teens who have been diagnosed with other mental illnesses that cause psychotic behavior, such as schizophrenia, may be more susceptible to psychotic depression. At times, it can be difficult to diagnose the difference between psychotic depression and a psychotic episode brought on by another mental illness. Usually, psychotic episodes from psychotic depression will be centered around the symptoms of depression. For example, the breaks in reality or the delusional thoughts will be centered on feelings of worthlessness.

Additionally, a single episode of psychotic depression or irregular episodes may be diagnosed as bipolar disorder instead. Having a psychotic depressive episode can increase the chance of developing bipolar disorder and of experiencing manic episodes later in life.

As with bipolar disorder, psychotic depression is often treated in multiple ways, addressing both the depression as well as offering treatment for the psychotic behavior. Antipsychotic medication is often used alongside an antidepressant to treat both aspects of this disorder.

Psychotic depression frequently leads to self-harm behaviors, hospitalization, and thoughts of suicide, so it is imperative that teens be given treatment as soon as possible. Often, teens may be confused or ashamed of these episodes; they may not properly recall what happened, or they may be afraid that they'll be accused of making it up.

Adults and caregivers of teens should pay close attention to talks of behavior that could be considered illogical or psychotic, especially when it occurs at the same time as symptoms of depression.

Substance-Induced Mood Disorder

Substance-induced mood disorder is actually a group of depressive disorders that are directly caused by the effects of substances. These substances don't have to be illegal drugs or alcohol; they can be medications prescribed for another illness, over-the-counter medications, or stimulants that would normally be considered healthy or even essential.

Substance-induced mood disorder can be caused either by taking a specific substance or by ceasing to take the substance. If a teen broke a bone, for example, and took pain relievers during the healing period, they could develop depression due to the pain reliever either at the start of the treatment or after stopping the medication.

This type of depression often includes bouts of depression followed by bouts of mania. Symptoms of mania and depression can appear simultaneously or the teen may cycle through the symptoms of one and then the other. This may mean that the teen is extremely energetic, restless, or engaging in risky behaviors at first and later is very lethargic, apathetic, and uninterested in doing anything.

Substance-induced depression can lead to self-harm behaviors and thoughts of suicide. In many cases, this type of depression is treated by focusing on the cause, which is the substance the teen is either taking or has stopped taking. If the substance is a prescription or an over-the-counter medication, the medication will likely be changed, and new treatment will be sought for the condition requiring the medication.

If the substance is a recreational drug or another dangerous substance, substance abuse treatment may be necessary. In either case, the treatment may be enough on its own, or it may need to include antidepressants to help a teen start to feel better. It's important for teens to be totally honest with doctors or nurses about the medications they use and any recreational substances they may use even occasionally. Doctors need this information to ensure they don't prescribe a medication that could cause depression and so that they can properly treat depression.

Postpartum Depression

This may not be a type of depression that many adults think of when they think of teenagers, but the fact is that teen mothers are twice as likely as adult mothers to suffer from postpartum depression for a myriad of reasons. Not only can this type of depression be dangerous for the teen, it can be dangerous for the new baby.

Postpartum depression is a depressive disorder that is brought on after childbirth. There are many things that happen during and after childbirth that can lead to depression:

- Hormonal changes.
- Extreme fatigue and sleep deprivation.
- Psychological adjustments to motherhood.

Medications the teen may be on as a result of the birth, frustration when things like breastfeeding don't go well, social concerns and bullying, and standard teenage bodily changes can cause or contribute to postpartum depression.

If a teen who has recently given birth is experiencing any of the following feelings, thoughts, or symptoms, she should be given medical attention:

- Being extremely overwhelmed and unable to cope with caring for an infant.

- Having guilt for not feeling happy about having a new baby.
- Not feeling bonded or connected to the new baby.
- Experiencing confusion, irritability, anger, or fear more than any other emotion.
- Being either unable to eat or eating an unhealthy amount at every meal.
- Thinking about running away or abandoning the baby.
- Being unable to stop the mind from racing.
- Having a sense of dread or frightening thoughts that make it difficult to leave the house.

Just as with other types of teen depression, postpartum depression can lead to self-harm behaviors, suicidal thoughts, and other serious consequences. There is also a risk that the teen may neglect or harm the infant.

It is important to realize that this happens because of the illness and not because the teen is a bad person or a bad mother. Steps should always be taken to help teens manage their depression and to support them in motherhood before other options are considered.

In Summary

There are many, many types of depression that can affect teens. These nine types are some of the most commonly seen, and depending on a teen's specific life situation, one type may be more likely than another.

By understanding the main symptoms of depression and how these symptoms can be obscured by other symptoms due to the many types of depression, it makes it easier to recognize depression and get treatment faster. We discussed these types of depression:

- Major depression, which is depression that exhibits extreme symptoms for at least two weeks.
- Dysthymia, which is depression that may be milder in severity, but lasts months or years.
- Bipolar disorder, which is a depressive disorder characterized by cycles of depressive behavior and manic behavior.

- Seasonal affective disorder, which is depression that comes on only during certain seasons (typically winter).

- Atypical depression, which is depression that looks like major depression, but the mood can be lifted by positive situations or circumstances.
- Premenstrual dysphoric disorder or PMDD, which is a depressive disorder triggered by the onset of the menstrual cycle.
- Psychotic depression, which is depression that is accompanied by psychotic symptoms and behaviors.
- Substance-induced mood disorder, which is depression related to the use of medications, drugs, alcohol, or other stimulants.
- Postpartum depression, which is depression related to giving birth.

In the next chapter, we'll discuss one of the most dangerous leading causes of depression in teens: bullying and social situations. This cause of depression has led to a shocking number of teen suicides and injuries. Learning how to address this cause could be a key to reducing the rate of teen depression across the country.

Chapter Three: Bullying is More Than Just Words

When adults hear the word bullying, they probably think back to a time in middle school or high school when they were ridiculed for their thick glasses or made fun of for the way they tripped in gym class or any other reason. Because most people went through some kind of bullying in school, they think of bullying as common and normal high school and middle school behavior that every child goes through and experiences.

The idea that bullying is normal is further seen in TV shows, movies, and books, where the teen bully is just another part of the daily life of a student. Teachers and parents don't seem to do much to stop the bully, or if they do, the solution is only temporary. In many cases, these bullying situations are played for laughs, showing that bullying is ultimately something to brush off.

Although bullying may seem commonplace in schools, the truth is that it should not be accepted as something that is normal. Being tormented, made fun of, and ostracized is certainly not fun for the victim, but it goes beyond hurt feelings and being lonely. The rise of depression and suicide in teens has a direct link to the way we treat bullying and how social connections are formed in the teen years.

In chapter three, we will take you into the world of bullying and how it can fuel teen depression. We'll look at why bullying and social problems can lead to suicide, and how the Internet changed the way bullying and depression are linked.

Finally, we'll discuss some of the things health care professionals and adolescent psychiatrists recommend for handling bullies and other social problems in high school.

What Are Bullying and Cyberbullying?

Before you can truly understand what teens go through, you must understand the difference between bullying and cyberbullying. Both types occur in school and outside of school at an alarming rate, and if teens cannot escape the ridicule, they may fall deeper into depression.

Bullying is characterized by behavior that is aggressive and unwanted by other teens in their school, grade, or social group. Those who are bullied view the bully as someone who has more power than they themselves do.

For instance, if a teen is bullied by a student who is popular and has many friends and connections, the bullied teen may feel like the bully is able to ruin their life by cutting off their chances at making friends or participating in activities comfortably.

For behavior to be considered bullying, it must occur on a regular basis. Someone who bullies another may spread rumors about the individual, speak badly about the person's family or friends, make harmful threats, physically attack the teen, and even exclude the teen from other social groups in school. All of these examples fall into one of the three types of bullying:

- Verbal bullying, which relates to anything that is said. This can include verbal attacks, sexual comments, threats, name-calling, and so on.
- Social or relational bullying, which relates to anything that hurts someone's reputation or relationships. This includes spreading rumors, excluding the teen from groups or activities, embarrassing the teen in public settings, telling others to exclude the teen, and so on.
- Physical bullying, which relates to anything done to a person's body or possessions. This can include physical

attacks, tripping the teen, breaking or stealing their things, and so on.

On the other hand, cyberbullying is a form of bullying that is done through the use of electronic media, typically social media, text messages, or chatrooms. When cyberbullying takes place, the bully may ostracize the victim and post things about them online that are untrue or are designed to make them feel bad about themselves. The bully may also post personal identifying information about the victim in a public space, such as revealing the victim's home address, full name, or other such information.

One of the reasons cyberbullying is such a fast-growing phenomenon is that it can be (and usually is) totally anonymous. There have been many studies on both teen and adult behavior that have consistently shown that we as humans are far more willing to inflict pain if we believe the victim does not know who we are. It can be impossible to track anonymous user accounts on many of the most popular social media sites that teens use.

Additionally, the nature of many of these sites means that content often is "evergreen." This means that once a user has made a comment, uploaded a mean photo, or in some way bullied someone, it can be nearly impossible to fully delete the message.

Other users can copy the message through reblogging, retweeting, screen capping, or other recycling methods. The more the content is shared or commented on, the stronger the archive of the content becomes. Soon, eradicating every trace of the bullying content can become totally impossible.

A phenomenon observed in both adult and teen Internet users is that of the "pile on" or herd-like behavior that can quickly create a huge spiral of bullying. This occurs when a person who is generally well liked or respected online posts content that disparages or shames another person. They could have what looks like a good reason for their content; perhaps the person they are targeting sent them a rude private message or did something even worse.

What follows is that all of the original poster's friends and followers, and ultimately their friends and followers, begin adding to the conversation. They add more evidence that the target is bad, they publicly condone bullying the target in other forums, and the crowd of hate can spiral out of control in mere minutes. If the target is an innocent victim of bullying, the person could literally log in to their favorite social media website after school to find thousands of messages, notifications, and mentions all sending one message: you are hated.

A teen who becomes a victim of cyberbullying may feel trapped and afraid to even look at their phone or the Internet. Cyberbullying can take place without the victim being bullied on school grounds. For instance, a teen may receive threatening and demeaning texts and instant messages, but they may not hear anything from the bully while at school.

Cyberbullying takes place twenty-four hours a day, seven days a week. Many teens are unable to escape it, and they find that they must give up things they love such as playing on the Internet or even opening their phone to call a friend. Because the bullying never stops, a teen can feel stuck in a never-ending cycle of ridicule.

The Connection Between Bullying and Suicide

Bullying is a serious problem and needs to be regarded as such, especially since it has a negative impact on teens. It is important to note that bullying and teen suicide are closely related according to many hundreds of studies performed by universities, the Centers for Disease Control (CDC), medical groups, and other organizations. But while a correlation is present, the extent of the correlation is unknown.

One of the reasons that the correlation is not readily known and available is because there are many teenagers who are bullied, but they do not all commit suicide. Many times, those teens who do commit suicide are not just bullied, they are also experiencing other types of issues, such as depression, anxiety, or other mood disorders.

Although studies are not conclusive that bullying itself leads directly to suicide, there is enough evidence that connects the two, so it is vitally important for parents and school boards to understand how dangerous bullying can be and to make help readily available.

Some specific factors can influence when teens may take a step toward suicide after they have been bullied. These are some of the influences and factors:

- Slower social and learning development.

- Family conflicts and issues.
- Stress or emotional distress.
- Substance abuse.
- Violent relationships, physical abuse, or sexual abuse.
- Lack of support or ways to cope.

One of the best ways to help teens cope with depression, suicide, and bullying is to sit down and speak with them. Teens need to know that there are resources to help them and there are ways to handle the situation to stop the bullying from occurring. Just as with depression, if a teen is reluctant to speak to a teacher or parent about bullies, seeking out an objective counselor could be the best option to ensure the teen is getting the necessary help.

As a parent, learning which websites your teen hangs out on and may be bullied on could be impossible. A website that's popular today could be replaced by the next thing tomorrow. The sudden and marked popularity of sites like Snapchat prove just how easy it is for a social media website to become the next best thing overnight. Teaching teens safe Internet habits and monitoring their behavior for signs of depression is ultimately going to lead to a better situation.

These are steps that adults and teens can take to help the victim cope with the effects of bullying. Of course, the bullying behavior should be addressed with the bully, their parents, and the school board as well. The information in this book is intended to focus only on the connection between bullying and depression.

Suicide Warning Signs

Whether or not you believe a teen is suicidal, you need to be prepared and know the warning signs. Not all teens will open up to their parents or guardians, and they may be very adept at hiding the fact that they have depression. Knowing what to look for will help you protect your child or another teen should they begin to exhibit signs that suicide may be on their mind.

Of course, you cannot expect teens to jump right out and say they want to commit suicide. They are unlikely to tell you they have even contemplated the idea at any point in their life. Because of this, the burden falls on parents and other caregiving adults to know when teens are silently calling out for help. Learn the subtle cues below and get teens the help they need immediately.

On the contrary, some teens will admit that they want to commit suicide, and they will express that they do not want to live or they would be better off dead. Some teens may even tell a close friend that they plan to end their life. In these situations, it is important to get them help right then and there.

Before we go over the suicide warnings signs, it is vital that you never shrug off any talk of suicide. Some teens who say they will commit suicide will not actually follow through, but that does not mean you should ignore the person. You never know just when someone is being truthful and trying to cry out for help before they take the plunge.

Here are some of the warning signs of suicide:

- A complete change in mood or appearance.
- Talks about suicide or ending one's life.
- Steps toward self-harm.
- Completely withdrawing from the outside world.
- Internet searches about suicide, how to commit suicide, and the like.
- Obtaining a gun, knife, pills, or another weapon to injure themselves.
- Writing a suicide note.

- Mentioning their pain and suffering will soon be over.
- Giving away personal belongings.

Before a teen commits suicide, you may begin to notice they are harming themselves and causing damage to their body. The type of self-harm a person does will depend on their pain threshold and what makes them feel comfortable and good inside.

Let's look at some of the most common types of self-harm:

- Cutting.
- Ripping out hair.
- Burning the skin.
- Carving into the skin.
- Trying to overdose.
- Eating disorders.

If a teen is showing signs of self-harm or suicide, talk to them and get them the help they need immediately. Don't wait two days or a week. Do it now. You can save a life.

Why Suicide?

If you are a parent, you may spend some time racking your brain trying to figure out why the teen you've always known as your happy child may have even contemplated the idea of suicide. You must remember that it is not something you did wrong, and the reason your teen is seeking suicide is because they are looking for a means to escape pain—whether this is because of bullying or another cause of depression.

When you think about suicide, you may think of someone who wants to die. This way of thinking is one of the largest misconceptions about suicide and it takes some understanding to truly get down to the real reason.

A teen who commits suicide likely does not want to die but sees no other way out. Teens turn to suicide to end their emotional, physical, or mental pain; to escape the depression; and to just stop everything.

All of their new responsibilities, changing schedules, and pressure to succeed and start planning for the future can add up quickly. In a teen's mind, suicide is the only way to make everything go away. Failed attempts to get help or stop the bullying by themselves have not worked and suicidal teens feel like their hands are tied.

Shocking Statistics on Bullying and Cyberbullying

To put things into perspective, it helps to look at some statistics that show just how bullying and cyberbullying happen in today's world. When you think about teen depression, bullying, or even suicide, you may think it doesn't happen that often and the numbers are just not there.

While it would be nice for the numbers to be low, they are actually at an alarming all-time high, which is quite scary:

- According to reports from the CDC, suicide is considered the third top cause of death in teens.
- This works out to a large number of 4,400 deaths every single year in the United States.
- The CDC goes on to say that for every one suicide that occurs, there are roughly one hundred attempts.

- The same study also shows that roughly 14 percent of all high school students have, at some point, considered suicide and 7 percent of all high school students have attempted it.
- Studies have also shown that students who are bullied are as much as nine times more likely to commit suicide than students who are not bullied.
- The National Crime Victimization Survey, which includes students in grades nine through twelve, reported that an estimated 2.2 million teens experienced some form of cyberbullying in 2011.
- The number of students who experienced cyberbullying rose by roughly 3 percent from the same study done in 2009.
- Recent reports from 2014 showed that 25 percent, or one in four students, have experienced ongoing bullying through the Internet or their cell phone.
- An astonishing 11 percent of teens have said that the cyberbullying they endured came from photos taken of them without their consent or knowledge.
- One of the most shocking statistics from 2014 revealed that 95 percent of teens who witnessed some form of cyberbullying on the Internet or social media did not say anything and simply ignored the behavior.

- Another eye-opening discovery revealed that over half of students said they never trust or confide in their parents about cyberbullying when it happens to them.
- In addition to cyberbullying and suicide, roughly 28 percent of all students in the United States from grades six to twelve have reported being bullied; 20 percent of those students are in grades nine to twelve.

These statistics are shocking, to say the least, and they truly put things into perspective. When looking over these studies and surveys, you may begin to panic and worry that your child is being bullied. It is important for you to speak to your child about bullying and let them know that you are there for them and ready to talk whenever your child wants to.

Bullying remains much more prevalent in school systems, but what is more concerning is the number of students who witness it and do nothing about it. Students refuse to report anything in fear of retaliation or being bullied themselves.

Another shocking discovery in the statistics shows that students are moving from traditional bullying into cyberbullying. The problem with cyberbullying is that teens are unable to escape this type of bullying, and it can go on nonstop twenty-four hours a day, seven days a week.

If you believe your child is experiencing any type of bullying, whether it be on school grounds or the Internet, get them the help they need and put an end to it.

In Summary

In this chapter, we looked at the difference between bullying and cyberbullying and how the classic picture of bullying as "just a part of growing up" is actually a very dangerous way to leave teens vulnerable to depression.

Bullying is unwanted aggressive behavior that happens repeatedly over a period of time. It can be verbal, physical, or social or any mixture of the three. Cyberbullying is behavior that happens online or via phone or other technology that targets someone and makes the person feel weak or hated.

Both of these types of behaviors are far more prevalent than parents and school officials realize. In this chapter, we shared some shocking statistics that show how bullying links directly to depression and suicidal behavior, as well as the sad numbers behind how prevalent teen suicide really is.

The correlation between bullying and depression could be a deadly one. It is vital that in addition to learning how to deal with the bullies themselves, we also learn how to offer the right kind of treatment for those who have been bullied.

In the next chapter, we'll take an even closer look at some of the statistics behind depression in teens.

Chapter Four: The Numbers Behind Teenage Depression

Depression may be a difficult subject matter to deal with, but it is important to face it head-on, especially as the numbers continue to rise year after year. More and more teens are depressed, experiencing bullying, and having trouble coping with their hormones and emotions.

We've shared quite a few numbers and studies throughout the chapters of this book, but in this chapter, we'll really dive into the many facts that show just how important dealing with depression is.

If you are a parent, although you may not fully understand what your child is going through, it is essential that you try to learn what depression is and what you can do to help your teen so that he or she does not feel all alone in this battle. These facts can help you to understand that you did not fail as a parent, your teen isn't just going through a "teenage phase," and you can gain the confidence you need to approach a doctor about your teen's treatment.

For teens, this chapter can help you realize that you are far from alone, you are not simply going through "normal teenage changes," being happy and content in life is truly normal, and it is completely necessary that you seek help in order to live the happy and content life you deserve.

Treating depression can be a simple, easy process—but first, you have to get the treatment. You can use these numbers and statistics to give yourself confidence when speaking to your parents or doctor.

Armed with the knowledge you will receive from these numbers, you'll be able to take the right steps toward helping yourself or helping a teen you care for to get the necessary help.

Get to Know the Numbers

In this section, we will talk about the statistics and get down to the numbers that show how many teens actually suffer from depression. We already saw the suicide and bullying statistics, and those numbers may have taken you aback.

Until recently, teens who suffered from depression were just labeled as moody or hormonal teens. Although this may sometimes have been the case, many others who actually needed an intervention were skipped over.

The true statistics of teen depression alone are startling:

Studies have indicated that roughly one out of every five children will have some sort of behavioral, mental, or emotional issue. When putting that into focus, it means if your child was in a class of twenty-five students, five of them would be at risk for having a mental, emotional, or behavioral disorder.

One in every eight teenagers suffers from depression at some point during their teen years. This means that in our example class of twenty-five, three or four would have depression.

One shocking number shows that an estimated 20 percent of all teens will experience some type of depression before they become an adult. Studies also showed that teen girls have a higher risk of developing depression when they lose their social status, friends, or any other factors including their school and social life. The study continues to say that boys are not likely to admit they have depression, and they do not seek out help even when they know there is a problem.

The Real Guide to teenage Depression

As a matter of fact, only roughly 30 percent of students who struggle with a disorder actually seek out help. The remaining 70 percent try to handle the situation on their own and simply deal with it. This means that in our class of twenty-five in which three had depression, one of those students *might* seek out help. It is likely that none of them would.

According to the National Institute of Mental Health (NIMH), 2.2 million teens ages twelve to seventeen experienced at least one major depressive episode in 2012. By 2014, that number had jumped to 2.8 million. By the time of this book's writing in 2016, nearly three million teens will have experienced at least one major depressive episode in the past year.

It takes approximately twenty weeks, or five months, of psychotherapy treatment to properly treat a standard case of depression. If the condition is more serious or is a part of another illness, like psychotic depression, the treatment could take far longer. In fact, the annual cost of health care directly related to depression in the United States is over 80 billion dollars.

Suicide is the third most common cause of death for teens between the ages of twelve and eighteen. If you extend the numbers to age twenty-four, due to the fact that the prefrontal cortex isn't fully mature until twenty-five, suicide is actually the second most common cause of death. Of these suicides, more than 90 percent of the teens who committed suicide were suffering a mental health problem.

Most commonly, firearms are used by teens to commit suicide. Over 45 percent of teens turn to firearms, with another 40 percent using suffocation, and 8 percent turning to poisoning or overdosing to commit suicide. Although girls tend to be more susceptible to depression, boys are far more likely to commit suicide; over 81 percent of the yearly reported suicides are among males.

Additionally, Native American and Alaskan Native teens have the highest rates of reported suicidal thoughts. Hispanic teens, however, are the most likely group to attempt suicide. And teens who identify on the LGBTQIA spectrum are four times more likely than their peers to attempt suicide.

Over 1.8 million teens who experience depression each year consider suicide. It is estimated that 5,400 teens attempt suicide every day in the United States. Of those 5,400, at least 4,320 of them gave multiple clear warning signs that could have been noticed by parents or teachers if they had known what to watch for.

By the time teenagers reach the age of eighteen, around 11 percent of them have a chronic depressive disorder. Every single year, more than 157,000 teenagers receive medical care for self-inflicted injuries.

More than 15 percent of teens who experience depression in their teen years develop bipolar disorder later in life. Teens who do have depression are far more likely to suffer from multiple episodes of depression before reaching adulthood rather than only suffering one or two episodes. While only 5 percent of the total American population suffers from depression at least once a year, 8.3 percent of the total teenage American population suffers from depression at least once per year.

As you can see, the numbers are quite shocking. They are a wake-up call for parents everywhere. If you believe that your teen is experiencing any type of depression or emotional problems, speak with them and try to get to the bottom of it. Throughout some of the studies, teens admitted that they do not tell their parents. Other studies showed that parents do not recognize when their teen is depressed.

Even if your child appears to be happy, "just moody," or all right, you need to let them know you are there for them and to keep an eye on their behavior. Below, we will discuss some important facts about teenage depression.

Important Facts about Teenage Depression

As a parent, now it is time to go over some of the facts about teen depression that you need to know. Remember, depression is more than just a bad mood or a stint of irritability. Many teens who experience any form of depression feel like they are alone and have no one to talk to or no one who will understand them. By learning more about the condition and reaching out to your adolescent, you can help him or her through this difficult time.

One of the most helpful things you can know and understand about depression is that it can be treated and almost all individuals who go through treatment will be able to better manage their condition and overcome their thoughts and feelings. Getting your teen help right away can prevent self-harm, reckless behavior, and even suicide.

Teens are not always going to open up to you about depression, and that is something you must understand. You can talk to your teen and let them know that you are there for them and give them the emotional support they need.

When you do begin talking to your teen about depression, try to avoid saying potentially upsetting things such as "Why do you act like this?" or "Why can't you just stop?"

Your teen wants more than anything not to feel like this, but feeling depressed is not your teen's fault, and there is no switch to just turn off those emotions.

Another thing to know is that depression is considered a serious problem and a mental disorder that needs to be treated. Anyone who goes through depression needs to seek professional care.

Studies have indicated that teens who have a family history of depression are more likely to experience depression themselves. In fact, parents who believe they are always knowledgeable about what their child feels are oftentimes wrong. Parents do not always know when their teen is having a bad day because some teens mask it and keep it hidden.

How to Talk to Your Teen about Depression and Suicide

We've looked at the facts so that you can improve your knowledge of teen depression and suicide rates. And we've explored the signs and symptoms you should watch for. We've discussed many times how important it is to talk to a teen about depression or any thoughts of suicide.

Your next question is probably: how do I do that? If you are like most parents or teen caregivers, you know that it's not always easy to simply sit down and talk. Teens need a lot of privacy as they grow and learn who they are, and they may not be willing to discuss what they feel are private internal failures with you. So what can you do if you believe a discussion needs to happen?

Or, alternatively, how do you approach the conversation if the teen comes to you first? If a teen confides in you that they are feeling depressed or suicidal, you as the adult they've trusted with this information have to be ready to offer the best conversation you can—one that leads to getting professional help. Here are some tips for having these conversations:

- Be sure you are listening. The most important part of this conversation is that the teen feels validated and that you are giving them all of your attention. Be sure that your body language is engaged, that you aren't using a phone or a computer at the same time, that you are asking questions and repeating back what you understand. All of these things show that you are actively listening.
- On the same note, validation is very important. Never tell a teen who tells you they are depressed or thinking about suicide that those are normal feelings for their age. Even with naturally occurring teenage changes, depression and suicidal thinking are not normal. The worst that could happen is that a doctor confirms the teen really isn't depressed; but even in this situation, you have still validated the teen's trust in you by believing them until a professional proves otherwise.
- Don't become anxious or "freak out." This conversation is about the teen and how they feel. As the adult, you must keep your emotions and reactions in check. Even if you feel as though they are blaming you for their

depression, or if you fear your child may try to take their own life, you cannot go on the defensive or turn into an overprotective parent. This puts the focus on you, which is not the point. Instead, calmly help the teen determine the best and most immediate course of action. Don't delay getting treatment (not even overnight), but do keep your calm.

- Be sure that you ask plenty of questions. Teens may have a hard time opening up about being depressed, and they may cover up just how deep the depression really goes. Ask them to explain or give examples whenever you can so that the true nature of the depression is understood.
- Let teens have input on their treatment. These are people who we expect to choose a vocation or a college major that shapes the rest of their lives, after all. They should be able to have some say in the doctors they see, the medications they take, and what other treatments they follow.

This is important not only to allow them autonomy, but also because some treatments may increase suicidal thoughts; if teens know they have input in the process, they will be more likely to point out a negative reaction instead of allowing it to fester.

- Consider alternative communication methods. If your teen suffers from anxiety or doesn't "do" face-to-face communication very well, how else can you communicate with them about their depression or suicide? Maybe they will be more comfortable e-mailing or texting. Perhaps some sort of code can be developed that parents and teens can use to let each other know when depressive behaviors or thoughts have been noticed.
- Be sure that you understand the risk factors. While all teens of any lifestyle, gender, sexuality, race, background, and the like can become depressed, there are certain risk factors mentioned in the statistics earlier in this chapter.

  If your teen is female, Hispanic, Native American, on the LGBTQIA spectrum, or is taking other medications or has another illness, it is far more likely that the teen will be depressed. Knowing this can help you realize that you aren't to blame, and neither is your child.
- Begin talking to your teen about their behavior, thoughts, and feelings early in life. Even if your teen is a happy, content person who shows no signs of depression at all, make a point of becoming comfortable discussing these things now. This can ease the way later,

so that if there is ever a need to discuss depression or suicide, your teen will be well versed in identifying and talking about their feelings.

- Find some support for yourself, but remember to keep it private. Yes, you will need support. Being the caregiver of a teen who is contemplating suicide is terrifying and difficult. But remember that when you are talking to your teen, it should be about them. Your support group is where you can focus on your own needs and thoughts about the treatment and healing process.

In Summary

This chapter was filled with a lot of statistics that can help you approach depression with a more analytical eye. We also discussed a few more things that parents in particular need to understand about teen depression and suicide, as well as practical ways that you can talk to a teen about depression and suicide.

In the next chapter, we'll put a spotlight on how depression can specifically affect teens who fall outside the realm of society's current norm, such as those with disabilities, those on the LGBTQIA spectrum, minorities, or those with other disorders.

These groups of teens have a higher risk of depression and suicidal thinking, and Chapter Five will discuss why that is, how social structures within high schools perpetuate behavior that worsens depression among these teens, and what we as a culture can begin doing to help these teens live to be healthy and happy adults.

Chapter 5: Depression and the Idiosyncratic Teen

While we have come very far as a society in accepting those who don't fit the average view of "typical," there is still a disparity between the services offered to most teens and the services offered to those who fall outside the norm.

Our understanding of depression in teens who are of a minority race or have disabilities or other mental disorders or fall on the LGBTQIA spectrum is much less than our understanding of teens who are white, neurotypical, from middle-class to upper-class families, heterosexual, cisgender, and able-bodied.

In part, this is due to the way that scientific research into depression has been conducted in the past. Many times, depression studies are performed by universities in areas where these populations are the largest. Because of now-outdated ideas of segregation and medical care, much of the historic research that is relied on only addresses certain populations as well.

Therefore, it's important to understand that while depression in teens outside of this population is still the same basic illness, it can affect them in different ways, and it can be due to different causes. This is even more important because the rates of depression and suicide among teens in the following categories is much higher, statistically.

In this chapter, we'll look at just a few of the types of teens who could face higher chances of depression and suicide. This is by no means an exhaustive list, but it will give you a good idea of how depression can be an even bigger worry in certain situations. The goal should always be to understand the teen better and to ensure that they can access treatment specific to their needs.

For teens who fall into these categories, understanding that you may have a higher risk of depression can help you take the steps you need to find help. Whenever possible, look for treatment options that specifically address teens like you, those who share your race, gender identity, and so on or teens with disabilities or disorders. This ensures that you'll get treatment that works for your specific situation; in some cases, the standard treatment available for depressed or suicidal teens is not going to work for your specific life situation.

Patrice M Foster

Depression in Teens with Disabilities

The term "disability" covers a wide variety of conditions:

- Physical disabilities that require the use of mobility aids or wheelchairs.
- Deafness, blindness, or the impairment of another sense.
- Learning disabilities, such as dyscalculia or dyslexia.

There are many other types of disabilities, but these are some of the most common in teens today. Among teens with disabilities, there are two larger subgroups: those who have dealt with a disability since birth and those who developed a disability later in life due to injury, illness, or genetic onset.

Depression and Recently Developed Disabilities

It is normal for those who have developed disabilities later in life to suffer from depression. After being able-bodied, or having the full use of a particular sense, suddenly being unable to live the way you used to can have a profound effect on the mental state of a teen. Not only must they either give up or relearn to do many things they used to love, their future is also going to be very different from the life they may have envisioned.

When depression affects teens who have recently developed disabilities or were recently diagnosed with a learning disability, it can be due in large part to the stages of grief. They are mourning their old life, as well as the life they envisioned for themselves. So it is normal for a teen to go through the stages of anger, denial, bargaining, and so on, before finally reaching a state of acceptance. If depression becomes a part of this cycle, however, such teens may need medication, counseling, or other treatments to help them come to terms with their new lives.

It's also important to seek out support groups or organizations specifically for teens with similar disabilities. Seeing other teens coping with similar lives and thriving in those lives can be a great way to help prevent or treat depression. A teen who used to love sports and now requires a wheelchair may find inspiration in a wheelchair basketball league, for example.

Depression in Teens Born with Disabilities

While you may think that those who have adjusted to a disability since birth would be less likely to suffer depression related to the disability, that is far from the truth. As teens reach high school, it can be harder for them to accept that they can't always participate in the same things as their peers or that they have to take more care in choosing a college or a field of study than their peers.

Teens with disabilities can also suffer because of teasing and bullying. While bullying can and does happen to teens with many disabilities, it can be particularly difficult for teens with so-called invisible disabilities, such as learning disabilities. When teens get bad grades or are seen as "stupid" or "incompetent" because they have a learning disability that their peers may not know about, they can be ridiculed and made to feel as though they will never succeed. This can quickly lead to clinical depression.

Most studies show that up to 40 percent of teens with learning disabilities suffer from depression, and over half of teens with depression who commit suicide have a learning disability. Although there is a much higher risk of boys with depression committing suicide in the overall population of depressed teens, there is no gender disparity present in the studies of those with learning disabilities. Girls with learning disabilities are just as likely as boys to commit suicide due to depression. While it doesn't relate directly to teens, it's also interesting to note that younger children with learning disabilities are highly likely to suffer from depression, especially those in the eight- to nine-year-old age range.

But there's another relationship at work between depression and disability; it isn't just that disabilities can lead to depression but that depression can lead to disabilities as well. For example, remember in earlier chapters, we discussed how teens who faced depression have a much higher risk of developing bipolar disorder later in life? And that teens who did experience bipolar disorder often engaged in risky behaviors that could lead to injuries or illnesses? In both cases, the symptoms of depression could lead to a situation in which a teen develops a disability.

Depression in Teens with Other Mental Disorders

"Mental disorders" is another blanket term that could mean a huge number of things. Everything from autism to obsessive-compulsive disorder or schizophrenia could be housed under this term. Unfortunately, teens who suffer from a mental disorder or syndrome also have a much higher risk of depression.

Teens on the autism spectrum have been shown to have a 37 percent higher chance of developing depression than teens who aren't on the spectrum. Even though this could be due in part to other factors like medications, hormones, chemicals, and so on, a large part is due to the way the autistic brain functions when overstimulated. Being forced to attend a crowded school every day can be difficult for some autistic teens, particularly if they are discouraged from performing the "stimming" behaviors that help them handle overstimulation.

As teens get more and more overwhelmed, it can become easier for their brains to produce more of the stress hormone that leads to depression. This same pattern can be observed in many types of mental disorders, each uniquely related to the challenges of the mental disorder. If a teen who suffers from OCD becomes overwhelmed by racing thoughts and OCD-related anxiety, it can also trigger stress hormones and depression.

The most difficult part of treating teens with mental disorders for depression is that it can be hard to diagnose in the first place. In some cases, the symptoms of the mental disorder and the symptoms of depression can be hard to disentangle. For example, autistic teens may not show much emotion in their normal states, so it may be hard for parents to notice when they are not acting like themselves.

Some mental disorders cause teens to be selectively nonverbal or to have difficulty ever speaking. This can also make it difficult to get treatment because such teens won't be able to express their need for help or explain how they are feeling.

This means that parents, teachers, and other guardians have to take extra steps to be sure that they know and observe teens with mental disorders very well; it will take a keen eye to discern the possible symptoms of depression.

In addition to the symptoms of classic depression, teens with other mental disorders may begin to exhibit these signs:

- They may develop repetitive or compulsive behaviors, or these behaviors may worsen if already present.
- They may have more tantrums or exhibit aggressive behaviors.
- They may begin performing self-harming behaviors like biting their hands or wrists.

- They may become especially interested in or obsessed with death.
- They may begin to struggle with everyday tasks that they have previously mastered or excelled at.

Because teens with mental disorders often experience the world differently from teens without mental disorders, it's important that any depression treatment takes this into consideration. Seeking out a counselor with experience in both the mental disorder and teen depression is a good idea.

Other treatments may include medication, but this can be tricky if the teen is already taking other medications. In this case, it is important to watch the teen carefully for signs that the depression could be worsening due to the medication. Social skills training, social activities, mentors or tutors, or other alternative treatments may also be recommended.

Depression in Minority Teens

As our statistics in the last chapter showed, the teens with the highest chance of attempting suicide are minority teens—in particular, black, Native American, and Hispanic teens have a very high risk of depression and suicidal thinking.

The Real Guide to teenage Depression

Nearly 8 percent of all black youth meet the criteria necessary to be diagnosed with major depression, and suicide is the third leading cause of death among black teens. Native American and Hispanic teens have among the highest percentage of suicide attempts for all teens in any category.

Why are these teens so much more depressed than their Caucasian peers? There are many reasons that are part of a much deeper sociological issue. In part, it may be due to racism that is present across the country and in particular to the many events that have sparked controversy between minorities and the police over the most recent years. It may also be due in part to the higher percentage of minority teens who live below the poverty line.

One of the most important things to realize about depression in minority teens is that despite being one of the groups with the highest risk of suicide and depression, they have the least access to treatment. Studies going back as far as 2004 have shown that the treatment facilities and options available in areas where minority teens live are not as easily accessible as those located in primarily Caucasian areas.

While it can be hard to truly gather the data necessary to say how few minority teens actually receive treatment, the best information from a study in 2011 suggested that only 31 percent of Hispanic teens with depression ever get help, only 32 percent of black teens with depression ever get help, and only 14 percent of Asian teens with depression ever get help. This is compared to around 40 percent of Caucasian teens with depression who receive help.

Helping minority teens to find a doctor or therapist of the same racial or ethnic background can make them feel more comfortable opening up about their depression, but even if this is not available—any treatment for depression in minority teens should also take into account social pressure, the scary news surrounding minority adults and the police, and other societal factors like racism that can occur to these teens every day.

Depression in LGBTQIA Teens

LGBTQIA stands for "lesbian, gay, bisexual, transgender, queer, intersex, asexual." Even though there are many, many other gender and sexuality identifiers (such as pansexual, nonbinary, and so on), this term is used an umbrella term to cover any teen who falls somewhere outside the realm of cisgender (meaning people who identify with the gender they were assigned at birth) and heterosexual (meaning people who are sexually and romantically attracted to the opposite gender).

Teens who fall into the LGBTQIA category are more than four times likelier to become depressed than teens who do not fall into this category. And while there isn't enough data to accurately give a statistic, there is a strong suggestion that transgender teens have the highest chance of this group of becoming depressed. This seems to be true whether or not the transgender teen is taking hormonal therapy.

There are many reasons why an LGBTQIA teen may become depressed. One of the main reasons is bullying and a lack of acceptance. Often shame, humiliation, and isolation go hand in hand with coming out, particularly if the teen lives in a rural or conservative area.

Surveys have shown that of teens in this category, up to 80 percent report verbal harassment every school year, 40 percent report physical harassment, and as many as 60 percent say they do not feel safe at school due to their gender identity or sexuality.

LGBTQIA teens are also more likely to abuse drugs and alcohol, which can lead to depression in itself. Up to 30 percent of the LGBTQIA population in general abuses a substance compared to only 9 percent of the total American population. These ratios are echoed in LGBTQIA teens.

In addition to seeking out treatment specifically related to addressing the stigma attached to gender identity and sexuality, teens in this category may need to join a Gay-Straight Alliance or start one in their school to have a safe place to make friends. Educators, parents, and other caregivers should ensure that teens have a safe place where they can be themselves while they deal with depression.

Suicide is a major problem in the LGBTQIA teen community. Nearly 50 percent of these teens admit to considering suicide at least once, and those who come from families that don't support their gender identity or sexuality are more than eight times more likely to attempt suicide than those who have supportive families. In a community that is already four times more likely to consider suicide than non-LGBTQIA teens, that number is astronomically high.

In addition, every single instance of physical harassment or verbal abuse that an LGBTQIA teen faces increases their likelihood of engaging in self-harming behaviors by more than 2.5 times. Parents and guardians of teens who fit into this category need to be on high alert—even if teens have a great support system and live in an accepting area, they can still develop depression and be at a higher risk for dangerous behaviors.

In Summary

The statistics are very clear: teens who fall outside society's view of normal or typical have a much higher chance of developing depression and of attempting suicide.

In teens with disabilities, depression can be due to mourning their old life or due to bullying and feeling left out. In teens with mental disorders, depression can be triggered by the effects their disorder has on their brain chemicals, as well as bullying and feeling isolated. Minority teens and LGBTQIA teens have some of the highest rates of depression and suicide in the country.

In all of these cases, the focus should be on finding treatment that directly addresses the factors that set a teen apart. The entire medical team and support team should realize that traditional depression therapies may not work and unconventional help may be needed.

Finding or creating safe spaces where teens can connect with those like them is a very important part of helping these teens work through depression. School associations or associations within your religious group or other social activity can be a lifesaver for teens who don't feel as though they have any other place where they can simply be themselves.

In the next chapter, we'll go more in-depth with depression treatments for all teens. We'll also talk about how to create a family and school environment that can help prevent depression and how one can seek out support for themselves.

Chapter 6: Prevention and Treatment of Teen Depression

Throughout the book, you have learned what depression is, how bullying increases the chances of suicide, and also the warning signs and symptoms. In this chapter, we will go over ways to help prevent depression and the most commonly used treatment methods available to teens.

Fully knowing and understanding what a teen is going through is not always possible, but there are things that parents and guardians can do to better understand. For instance, reading this book is one of the first steps to better understanding depression and how it affects teens.

Many adults have never dealt with depression before, so this is uncharted territory for them. When you first recognize that a teen has depression or you have an idea that they may, it is important to sit down and begin talking to them.

We've shared some pretty frightening statistics in this book so far, but here's one that can give you hope: almost 90 percent of teens who undergo treatment for their depression are able to pull through and learn how to cope with the condition.

Seeking out treatment for a teen is truly the best way to help them—this isn't a condition that should just be left to resolve on its own. Teens can't simply walk it off. With the right treatment from medical professionals, teens will almost certainly heal and be back to their healthy lives.

Now, let's delve into ways that you can help prevent depression in teens.

Ways Parents Can Prevent Depression

When you find out that your teen child is depressed, you may begin to feel like you don't know what to do. As your adolescent slips further into depression, you may feel like you are losing them and you do not know how to get them back. The cycle can seem endless, but there are ways to prevent depression before it starts.

Studies have shown that depression begins to grab hold of a teen in their early years, many times by the age of fourteen. It is important for you to practice prevention and learn how to prevent depression before your child reaches this vulnerable age.

You are probably sitting here thinking about how you can prevent depression right now. It is not a foolproof method as there may be deeper issues that are bothering your child, but it is a step in the right direction.

Let's go over some ways that you can prevent depression in your teen.

1. Start a Relationship

Although your child may see you as the nagging parent, you should form a deep relationship with them based on lots of communication. This relationship will become essential when your teen does start to feel depressed or bummed out.

Your relationship with your child should focus on affection and communication. Your teenager wants to know that he or she is loved and you should tell them each day how much you appreciate and love them. Teens who do not feel loved may begin to spiral downward, especially if they see their friends receiving attention from their parents.

Communication is also essential; it lets your teen know he or she can confide in you. When it comes to communication, you do not have to invade your teen's life, but you can simply ask how their day was or about school, or you can start a conversation about a show the two of you are watching.

If you find that your teen does not want to talk to you, do not force the issue as this will only create negativity.

Another important part of forming a relationship is finding a shared interest that the two of you partake in regularly. It may be going to baseball games, visiting museums, attending pottery classes, or simply trading the funnies over breakfast every Sunday. Make it a routine, though. This gives you ample opportunity to observe your teen's behavior and opens dialogue with them about important matters, including depression or suicide.

2. Encourage a Healthy Lifestyle

Another great way to prevent teen depression is to encourage your child to have a healthy lifestyle. This includes getting enough sleep, eating better, and exercising. As your child becomes more involved in a healthier lifestyle, he or she will feel better overall and be able to focus and have much more energy.

This is especially important to help prevent the chances that a teen could develop other mood disorders later in life. The better health the brain is in now, the less chance there is of developing bipolar or other disorders. Not only can you help your teen survive their years as a high school student, you're also giving them a boost for the future.

Many studies have shown that exercise releases certain chemicals in the brain that can drastically improve mood, memory ability, interest in life, and overall well-being. In addition, there are many hundreds of studies that show that consuming too much sugar and artificial ingredients can actually stunt the proper growth of the young brain, making it harder for teenage brains to produce the appropriate amount of hormones and chemicals and leading to an imbalance.

For these reasons and many more, focusing on a healthy lifestyle is one of the most important tips on this list.

3. Set Rules and Define Consequences

When your child has guidelines and rules to follow, you are giving them responsibility and allowing them to make their own personal choices. Of course, you need to establish the types of punishment that will occur should your child act out or do something you do not approve of. Once you have made these guidelines and punishments, stick to them.

The reason that this can help prevent depression is twofold: first, it gives teens a framework for expectations, which helps them make better choices. If they know that substance abuse will be met with a severe consequence, they are more likely to think twice about using a substance that can lead to depression.

Second, it sets into place rules that prevent harmful behaviors from occurring in the first place. For example, if a teen is not allowed to be on the Internet for more than a set time every day, it will greatly reduce their chances of being cyberbullied.

4. Encourage Them to Do What They Love

Encouraging teens to participate in the activities they love will help them keep their minds off depression. For instance, if your teen loves to dance, encourage them to enroll in dance classes to help keep them busy and their mind from wandering. Not only will your teen love participating in a much-loved activity, they will be getting exercise meeting new friends.

One thing to keep in mind when it comes to encouraging your child is that you should not put too much emphasis on performance nor should you punish your child for failing as this will make them feel down and out. The focus should be on the teen's enjoyment of the activity and how the involvement makes them feel.

It's also important to consider what the activity is and what potentially harmful side effects it could have. If your teen is passionate about making movies and wants to upload them to YouTube, you may need to look into ways to prevent cyberbullying (such as disabling comments, having your teen's password for YouTube, or requiring that videos be screened by you before being uploaded to the Internet).

5. Good Support System

Just as communication is important, so is making sure teens have a good support system behind them. A support system can be made up of parents, grandparents, schoolteachers, counselors, friends, and more.

When teens have a team backing them up, they will know that they can confide in these people and they'll be more apt to speak with them about depression or problems that arise. In some cases, your teen may need to speak to someone else in their support system before they speak to you—they may feel as though they are letting you down by being depressed; maybe they fear adding to your stress if you are going through a trying time; or it could be that a teen relates more to another adult.

For example, if a young male teen is being bullied in the locker room, but his parent is a single mother, he may feel more comfortable speaking to his sports coach about the matter first. As a parent, the most important thing should always be that the teen is getting the necessary support, rather than that the teen is specifically talking to you.

Ways Educators Can Prevent Depression

There are many ways that educators can create classroom environments that help prevent depression. Because school is the place where teens spend most of their time, this is an important environment that cannot be overlooked. Here are some ways that you can make a classroom a place where depression cannot thrive:

1. Focus on Learning Rather than Performance

While all teachers have to follow the curriculum required by their state or area, there are still plenty of opportunities to focus on learning and engagement rather than performance. Allowing more self-chosen topics for essays, for example, or allowing classrooms to engage in more self-led debates, can be a great way to keep teens interested and curious about the topic. Focusing on problem-solving skills rather than memorizing tables of facts can be another way to shift the focus from performance.

The reason that this can help prevent depression is that in many cases, depression is often compounded by feelings of failure, intense pressure, or guilt about letting people down. If teens feel as though their job in the classroom is to be engaged every day and to learn new things that interest them rather than to prove that they know things, they are far less likely to feel that stress.

2. Pay Attention

With as many as two million teenagers going undiagnosed with depression every year, one of the best things any teacher can do is watch for the signs of depression. Remember, the student who seems like an uncooperative "problem child" may actually suffer from debilitating depression.

There are screening exams that can be given to students in class, especially in classrooms that have many high-risk students, such as minorities or LGBTQIA students. However, simply observing the behavior of students and watching for the signs of depression and any changes in behavior can be a great step.

3. Stop Bullying Before it Happens

If your school doesn't have an anti-bullying program in place that actively teaches kids how to deal with bullies and has clear consequences for bullying behavior, you need to address this with the principal or school board right away. In today's world, no school should ever be without a program of this nature.

The Real Guide to teenage Depression

Your program should focus on these areas:

- Ensuring that teens know how to remove themselves from a bullying situation.
- Ensuring that teens know whom they can approach when bullying occurs.
- Ensuring that teens know the specific consequences for bullying that happens on school grounds. There may also be a precedent for consequences if a student is caught cyberbullying, such as the inability to participate in extracurricular activities.
- Ensuring that teens know the facts and statistics about bullying and how it can lead to suicide.
- Ensuring that teachers are regularly refreshed on how to handle bullying when they observe it and if it is reported to them.
- Ensuring that parents are part of the program and understand all the consequences and resources for help as well.
- Ensuring that there is extra help in place for both the victims of bullies and the bullies themselves.

By putting a program in place, you'll make it far easier for your school to prevent bullying and to prevent the depression and possible suicide attempts that follow bullying in so many cases. You'll also make it easier to address bullying as you see it or hear about it.

4. Teach Students to Manage Stress

Teens are rapidly becoming adults, but they are still children, and as such, they don't always know exactly how to manage the feelings and responsibilities they now have. Essentially, the teen years are when children are suddenly given a lot of the same responsibilities and stresses that adults face every day, and this can be confusing and difficult. Just as adults have to learn to manage the stress of their jobs, families, marriages, and so on, teens need help learning to manage stress.

There are many ways that a classroom can be used to teach stress management. For example, teachers can emphasize the importance of ritual and how it allows the brain to transition from one thing to another. Always go over the previous day's chapter for the first two or three minutes of class, for example, and always give a brief introduction to the next day's chapter before the bell rings. Just by doing this simple routine, you help students understand how structuring their time can manage stress.

Another thing you can do as a teacher is to make time for quiet moments as your teaching schedule allows. Modeling mindfulness for your students helps them understand how being aware of your stress level and actively seeking to quiet your mind can help.

These activities can make a big difference in teens with depression, who may not ever see this sort of mindful behavior elsewhere. Talk to them openly about how structuring their homework time and taking mindful breaks can help them avoid depression and other illnesses.

5. Talk to Parents

Finally, teachers should always make sure they are part of the team of supporters for every teen they teach. Find a way to reach out to parents, through e-mail, social media, or conferences. Be proactive in talking to them about any concerns you have, or ask them if they have any concerns that you should watch out for.

The focus should always be on giving the teen every support option available. If your school offers extra help for depressed teens, such as guidance counselors who can be approached at any time, make sure that your teen students' parents know this. They can help encourage teens to take advantage of help.

Ways Teens Can Prevent Depression

This book isn't just for parents and caregivers. Teens also may need this information to learn more about what is going on inside themselves. For teens who may be facing depression or who are worried about someday facing depression, here are some things that you can do to prevent it:

1. Stay Connected

In many cases, isolation is one of the main causes and signs of depression. When you start to feel cut off from your family, friends, peers, or support group, it's easy for the other symptoms of depression to start sinking in. When depression does arise, almost everyone has a tendency to start withdrawing from activities or social groups.

However, one of the best ways to prevent depression from taking hold is to go against those instincts and to stay connected. Reaching out to friends, parents, teachers, or anyone else in your support group is not a sign of weakness; in fact, you are a very strong person for recognizing that you need the extra support and getting it.

Make sure you find ways to connect in person, rather than just over the phone or Internet. While these are good ways to connect with friends on a casual basis, there is something particularly uplifting to the brain and mood about meeting face-to-face. Even if you are an introvert, having a one-on-one meeting with someone who cheers you up can help the brain produce calming chemicals.

Likewise, you should always try to be there for your friends when they reach out to you for the same support. This boosts your own mood as well, making you feel good about yourself, so it's another good way to prevent depression. If your group of friends doesn't often reach out and you'd like to cheer yourself up by helping others, try looking for a volunteer position in a field that interests you.

Staying connected can also mean connecting with your pet. Many studies have shown that animals can be a big boost to our mental health. In fact, pet owners are less likely to suffer depression, heart attacks, stroke, and many other leading causes of early death.

2. Stay Healthy

Staying healthy is a very important part of preventing depression. There are three main things to focus on:

- Get plenty of exercise.

The brain releases multiple chemicals related to happiness during and after exercise. This is what causes the so-called "runner's high" that athletes get after a long run or other long workout. Workouts that are rhythmic and continuous like running (or swimming, dancing, martial arts, and weight training) can allow you to slip into this trance of feeling good.

However, it's also important to be mindful during your exercise, which can help you learn to better manage stress. Adding yoga to your routine can help, but even simply choosing to be aware of your body, your breathing, and your feelings during exercise is plenty. This allows you to become accustomed to identifying your emotions, which can make it easier to notice depression before it even begins.

- Get plenty of sleep.

Teenagers need more sleep than any other group of humans except newborn babies. As the brain and body are going through drastic changes during the teen years, your rest is very important. This is the time when your body and brain can both recharge and regulate the hormones and chemicals being produced.

Unfortunately, most teens have very busy schedules. In addition to being at school till at least three or four o'clock every afternoon, you may have extracurricular activity practice, a part-time job, religious activities, volunteer work, family time, social events to attend, homework to do, pets to care for, exams to study for, chores to perform, and a number of other demands on your time. All of these things can add up to a sleep-deprived teenager.

While it's not always easy to give things up, remember that depression can be life threatening if not prevented or treated right away. Your schedule may need to be rearranged, and some activities may need to be put aside while you get some rest. You may also need to use your study time more efficiently or try to find ways to combine certain activities, such as practicing speeches for debate team while you walk your dog, for example.

- Avoid sugar.

While eating better, in general, is a great way to keep your health at optimal levels, one of the key changes to make in your diet is to avoid sugar. Sugar has been shown to cause the brain to act in bizarre ways and can contribute to the imbalance of hormones that lead to depression.

Sugar also makes it harder for the body to keep blood sugar at the right level, which is more important than many people realize. When blood sugar is too high or too low on a regular basis, a person's mood and mental capabilities can be reduced drastically. Avoiding sugary drinks and foods and opting for honey or other natural sweeteners is a great way to help prevent depression.

3. Fake Enthusiasm till It's Real

One of the things that often happens when people are depressed is that they stop participating in things they love.

They don't feel any interest or enthusiasm for an activity anymore, and it becomes easier to find excuses not to participate. Pretty soon, they are withdrawing altogether, which only makes depression worse.

Instead of withdrawing, you can acknowledge that you aren't feeling enthused about something at the moment and fake it anyway. There is truth to the idea that you can "fake it till you make it." Scientific studies have shown that faking a smile can lead to a genuine feeling of happiness after only a few minutes. If you fake being happy, your brain will quickly become focused on the activity, and you'll forget you were faking in the first place.

Additionally, even fake enthusiasm is counted as enthusiasm by chemicals in the brain. If you teach your brain to associate an activity with a feeling of interest and excitement, you'll soon find that you no longer have to force the feelings. Your brain will naturally produce them.

If you just can't get beyond feeling unenthusiastic about an activity, find a new activity that you've always wanted to try, and use the small amount of interest you can muster up in that as a springboard. The key focus should be on doing things you love, however, not on things that are important for your resume or things that make someone else happy. Now is your chance to take a dance class just because you liked the movie *Step Up* or to start training to climb Mount Everest even if you think it'll never happen.

4. Challenge Negative Thoughts

When you are feeling depressed, oftentimes you'll find yourself becoming very anxious about upcoming events or things you have to do. Your mind will race from one thing to another, and you'll think to yourself that you will surely fail because you can barely focus on even one of those tasks.

When this sort of negative thinking occurs, one of the best ways to challenge it is to ask yourself, "What's the worst that can happen?" Be totally honest with yourself here. If you don't turn in your homework and you get a low grade, you may fail your class. Then you may have to take the class again next semester.

At the worst, you'll find yourself repeating a course that you don't love. Colleges and universities will still accept you, and you'll still be able to be successful in your career. In ten or fifteen years when you are busy with your adult life, you won't even remember what homework it was that you didn't turn in.

Another thing you can do to challenge negative thoughts is to remind yourself of the truth and keep a journal of evidence to prove the truth to yourself. If you think no one loves you, remind yourself of all the times your parents, friends, grandparents, or anyone has said that they love you. Look at pictures of you and your friends having fun. Ask your mom to tell you about the day you were born.

By actively considering each thought and reframing your worries or getting rid of the lies the depression is trying to tell you, you'll be one step closer to preventing the depression from taking hold.

5. Seek Out the Good

It can be easy to get caught up in seeing the bad all around us on a regular basis. If you are living in an area where scary things happen on the news, if your parents are getting a divorce, if you recently had a major life change, or if you are facing many other situations, you can get very bogged down in bad things.

It's a great idea to stop and look around for good things to cheer you up. Keep a journal of things that make you happy or things that were good about each day. Watch a movie that makes you laugh or invite your best friend over to play some video games or just hang out for no reason.

If you are having a really difficult time finding the good around you, talk to your parents. Maybe it's time for a family vacation, or maybe they'll be able to help you find a new way to look at things. Volunteering is another great way to find some good—being surrounded by people who care and want to help others can make you feel as though the world is a much brighter place.

This may also be a good time to get a pet if you don't already have one. Animals are predisposed to being happy because they cannot comprehend the bad things that we as humans see in the news and around us every day. As you take care of your pet, you'll find that some of their happy, carefree attitude can remind you of what is really important.

What matters most is that you do take the time in some way to seek out good things in life. This skill is important as an adult as well, so it's great to start cultivating it now. Once you've identified the good things around you, you may want to start considering how you can add to the good in your life. What can you do to make your mind, home, school, town, social group, or any other part of life better for those in it? By asking yourself these questions, you become an active part of seeking out your own happiness.

6. Don't Punish Yourself

Many times, depression leads us to feel as though we deserve to be sad. We are so focused on the bad things that are happening, on the way that we've hurt our friends by withdrawing, or on the way that we let others down when we quit activities, that we begin to believe we don't deserve to be happy.

It's this sort of thinking that can lead to self-harming behaviors. While most people instantly think of cutting when they hear "self-harm," it's only one method of one type of self-harm. There are other types of physical self-harm:

- Pulling out hair or picking at the skin until there are sores.
- Burning oneself.

- Forcing oneself to eat too much or too little or forcing oneself to vomit up food after eating.

Another type of self-harm goes on inside the mind. This occurs when teens force themselves to listen to their negative thoughts without challenging them. They hear depression tell them that they are worthless or unloved, and they accept it as the truth. This causes an extreme mental and emotional reaction that is every bit as harmful as cutting or other physical self-harm.

The important thing to understand is that these behaviors are an act of punishment. Teens believe they deserve to be in pain and punish themselves for being too weak to be happy, for letting others down, or for a myriad of other reasons. This behavior has to be stopped right away.

If you are depressed and you feel as though you are guilty of something terrible and should be punished for it, go back to the beginning of this book. Read about the scientific causes of depression, and understand that this is not your fault. You are not weak, and you have done nothing wrong.

7. Get Help

Finally, the last thing teens can do to prevent depression is to seek help the moment they suspect they may be getting depressed. Many teens may avoid this step. They may fear that they will be accused of seeking attention or that they will be ignored or dismissed. If you are good at acting happy and interested all the time, you may believe that your parents or caregivers couldn't possibly believe you.

But it's important that you keep trying to reach out to help. At the end of this chapter, you'll find a list of the hotlines and national treatment organizations that exist to help teens in need. If you cannot reach your parents, your teachers, your doctors, or anyone else and get them to help you with depression, reach out to one of those hotlines or organizations. They can help you find the right way to approach your parents and get the help you need.

Treatment Options Available for Teens

Depression is a condition that will eat away at a teen and cause him or her to become even more depressed. The longer the condition goes untreated, the more likely it is that a teen will begin to think about ways to escape from the pain, including suicide.

As a teen falls further into depression, you may notice that he or she begins to withdraw completely from the outside world and even from you. Keep in mind that you do not want to allow this to happen to your teen and you need to let them know that you are there for them.

Depression cannot be treated if you do not seek treatment for your child. The condition will not just disappear or wear off over time. Once you begin to notice the warning signs of depression, seek out immediate care for the teen in question.

When you take your child to the doctor, he or she will usually refer you to a social worker or case manager or psychiatrist who can provide services to your teen. The mental health professional that you go to should have experience working with teens who have depression.

If you do not seek out a specialist, you will find that treatment may not be working as effectively as it should be. Teens who go through depression do not have a cut-and-dry reason for the way they feel and someone who has experience in handling teen depression will know how to get to the bottom of your child's condition.

Individual and Group Counseling

One of the most common treatment methods for teen depression is individual and group counseling. Individual counseling allows your child's psychologist to understand them better and to speak with them on a personal level. This type of counseling is effective at finding the reason behind a teen's depression.

Group counseling is ideal for teens who need to know that they are not alone. Group sessions allow teens to meet with other teens the same age who are going through the same thing. During these counseling sessions, adolescents will have the opportunity to speak about their experiences and connect with each other.

Group counseling helps to build another support system for teens and provides another place where friendships can quickly form.

Treatment Using Medications

Medication is another common treatment method used to help teens cope with depression. Antidepressants are typically prescribed depending on how severe a teen's condition is. Many doctors rely on these medications to help teens focus and feel much better about their situations.

In addition to antidepressants, teens may be given sleep medications or medications that help them focus better in school. Whether or not a teen has an underlying condition will determine the additional types of medication he or she may receive.

If a teen is placed on medication, parents need to make sure they are monitoring when their teen takes it as missing a dose can lead to episodes of depression or manic depression. Teens who are diagnosed with bipolar disorder will have a change in attitude if they are not taking their medications.

As with any other medication, people can become dependent on antidepressants and these medications can increase suicidal thoughts in teens. If you notice that a teen is increasingly talking about suicide or begins to make comments about it, speak with the teen's health care provider about changing the medication.

Lastly, there are a number of other treatment options to help a depressed teen, including hospital care and even Cognitive Behavioral Therapy or CBT. During CBT treatment, the teen will undergo treatment that involves recognition of thoughts and actions and the relationship between the two. The goal behind CBT is to help the teen recognize the effects depression has on his or her life and why those feelings are there.

Treatment is effective when a teen receives the care he or she needs and parents need to seek out the right medical care for their teen to help them overcome depression and prevent suicide.

Seeking Support for Yourself

In an earlier chapter, we mentioned that the parents and caregivers of depressed teens will need their own support as well. When talking to your teen, the focus should be on them and on their feelings; but when they are being treated, you should also take a moment to consider your own mental well-being.

Being the caregiver of a person with depression can be difficult. It can be even harder if you are the teen's parent. You may find yourself exhibiting symptoms of depression, particularly insomnia, excessive anxiety, racing thoughts, and more as you contemplate the frightening statistics about teen depression and suicide.

Even if you are a single parent, you should be sure that you have someone you can talk to about the feelings you are having. If your spouse is not available, seek out a good friend or even a doctor or therapist. There are also group meetings for parents of depressed teens that can help you.

It's important to monitor your own behavior for signs of depression. If you begin to withdraw from activities and connections because you are depressed, your teen may no longer feel as though they can come to you with their worries or thoughts. This can leave your teen with no options other than to self-harm.

An additional good reason to seek out a support group or therapy is that it can offer you suggestions and tips that you may not have found elsewhere for talking to or monitoring your teen. Another parent of a depressed teen may say something that sparks an idea, and you and your teen may find that this idea is the perfect way to communicate about your teen's depression. Therapists often have excellent ideas for communicating better with your loved ones as well.

Hotlines and Treatment Organizations

This is by no means a full list of every hotline or teen depression organization there is. However, at the time of this writing, these are some of the best resources teens or parents of teens can use to help a teen with depression. All of these organizations have a focus on teen health specifically.

Crisis Call Center
800-273-8255 or text ANSWER to 839863
Twenty-four hours a day, seven days a week.
http://crisiscallcenter.org/

This website is intended to help anyone who is contemplating suicide or is in some kind of crisis. They operate a variety of crisis lines, all of which can be found under the menu at the top of their website. Some of these are specific to teens, some are specific to suicide, some are specific to substance abuse, and some cover much more. If you need help dealing with suicidal thoughts, this is a great place to start.

Depression and Bipolar Support

800-273-TALK (8255)

Twenty-four hours a day, seven days a week.

http://www.dbsalliance.org

This organization is intended to help anyone dealing with depression or bipolar disorder. They also cater to teens and children, and they have services for the parents of teens and children with depression or bipolar disorder. Their website can offer more information on the many educational resources they offer across the nation.

National Hopeline Network

800-SUICIDE (784-2433)

800-442-HOPE (4673)

Twenty-four hours a day, seven days a week.

http://www.hopeline.com

This organization is specifically focused on college-aged students but also helps teens with depression and suicidal thoughts. In addition to offering the hotlines, they also feature educational resources on their website that help teens learn more about depression and how to cope.

Crisis Center and Hotlines Locator by State

1-800-273-TALK

http://www.suicidepreventionlifeline.org/getinvolved/locator

This website makes it easy to find a crisis center or hotline specific to your area. Just type in your ZIP code, or search by your state on the home page to find the closest help center. You can also call the hotline listed above, and your call will be routed to the closest crisis center to your location.

Suicide Prevention Services Depression Hotline

630-482-9696

Twenty-four hours a day, seven days a week.

http://www.spsamerica.org

This organization is focused on helping teens and young adults get past feelings of suicide and move on to happy and healthy lives. They offer multiple counseling and educational services, as well as a hotline you can reach out to at any time.

Thursday's Child National Youth Advocacy Hotline

800-USA-KIDS (800-872-5437)

Twenty-four hours a day, seven days a week.

http://www.thursdayschild.org

This organization provides a variety of hotlines and information specifically aimed at kids and teens with depression. The website can be difficult to navigate, so the best option is to call the listed hotline for help.

The Trevor Lifeline

Specifically focused on LGBTQIA teens

866-4-U-TREVOR (488-7386)

Twenty-four hours a day, seven days a week; they also host a weekly live chat.

http://www.thetrevorproject.org

The Trevor Project is an organization specifically focused on helping LGBTQIA teens and young adults with feelings of depression or thoughts of suicide. They host weekly live chats and have a variety of communities around the Internet that teens can become involved in to make friends and find a safe space.

The Jason Foundation

Specifically focused on preventing teen suicide

1-888-881-2323 or 615-264-2323

Not monitored 24/7.

http://jasonfoundation.com/

This organization is designed to help teens who are considering suicide. They do not operate a hotline, but they do have a ton of great educational material and counseling options available. Once you've reached out to an emergency hotline and you want to find more information or help, this could be an excellent place to go. They also offer resources for parents that can be very helpful.

In Summary

This chapter covered many of the things you need to know about treatment and prevention of depression.

Parents can help prevent depression by creating a home environment that allows teens to feel comfortable approaching parents with their feelings and concerns. Starting a relationship built on communication early is vital as is enforcing smart rules and encouraging teens to participate in activities they are interested in.

Teachers can help prevent depression by focusing on creating a classroom environment free of bullying and filled with opportunities for teens to follow their passions.

Teens can do many things to keep themselves free of depression, including keeping their bodies healthy, attacking negative thoughts with the truth, and knowing that they do not have to punish themselves for feelings of guilt that are brought on by depression.

Treatments for depression include therapy, behavioral therapy, and medication, and will often include a combination of all three. Parents should be sure to seek support themselves as well, to ensure that they are able to offer the best support for their teen.

Finally, at the end of this chapter, we provided a list of many of the hotlines and treatment organizations that teens can seek out if they are in need. If you have ever struggled with depression or you feel as though you might be depressed now, please highlight that page, and reach out to someone. If you

The Real Guide to teenage Depression

aren't able to talk to your parents, teachers, or friends about the things you are feeling, the people on the other end of those phone numbers are there to help.

Parents, you can also use those hotlines yourself to seek help for your teen. If you don't know how to talk to your teen about depression and need a coach to guide you through the specifics, get in touch with places like the Trevor Project or the Jason Foundation for more help.

Conclusion

Teen depression is a serious condition as you have learned throughout this book. If the proper treatment is not sought for your child, he or she can begin to self-harm or even commit suicide.

A teen who feels left alone or has withdrawn from their peers is likely to fall into depression and be unable to find their way out.

Suicide is something that no parent wants to think about, but you must. If your teen is displaying any signs of suicide or begins to make comments about how they would be better off dead, they need immediate care.

Treatment for depression in teens is effective and can be done using counseling, medications, CBT, or a combination of multiple options. While treatment is effective, your child will also feel better if they know that you are by their side. No teen wants to go through this alone, and although they may show signs that they just want you to buzz off, they truly don't.

Parents should never give up on their adolescent, and learning about and understanding depression and how you can prevent it will help you provide care that matters to your teen.

Remember, you and your teen are not alone, and the shocking statistics and numbers show that. Before your teen becomes another statistic, intervene and help them get their life back now.

In this book, we went through the scientific causes of depression to show you that depression is no one's fault. It is the direct result of hidden functions in the brain, as well as a combination of social factors. We also talked about how depression affects the growing teenage brain specifically. We discussed a few of the many types of depression, and there are multiple lists throughout the book that can be used to watch for signs of depression. If you see a teen exhibiting at least two of any of the signs on these lists for more than a day or two, speak to them about how they are feeling. You can never know just how long the symptoms have been going on until you ask.

We also talked about bullying and cyberbullying and how these two things are linked to teen depression and teen suicide. The shocking statistics behind teen depression and suicide can help everyone understand just how serious depression really is for teens.

In another chapter, we discussed how teens who fall outside the societal norm can be more heavily affected by depression. Finally, we went over many ways to prevent and treat depression and provided a list of hotlines that anyone can use at any time to seek help.

If you know any teens who need help with depression, but you aren't their caregiver, consider offering them or their parents this book. You could help save a life.

Patrice Foster is a Registered Nurse of twenty-eight years. Located in the Greater Atlanta area, she provides advice for parents and teenagers on depression at her blog PatriceFoster.com.

Resources

WebMD; "Teen Depression," accessed November 22, 2016, http://www.webmd.com/depression/guide/teen-depression.

Alia Butler, "Effects of Teen Depression," accessed November 22, 2016, http://www.livestrong.com/article/161448-effects-of-teenage-depression/.

Mayo Clinic; "Teen Depression: Overview," accessed November 22, 2016,
http://www.mayoclinic.org/diseases-conditions/teen-depression/basics/definition/con-20035222.

"Parent's Guide to Teen Depression," accessed November 22, 2016,
http://www.helpguide.org/articles/depression/teen-depression-signs-help.htm.

"Depression," accessed November 22, 2016, http://teenmentalhealth.org/learn/mental-disorders/depression/.

Catherine Pearson, "Depression in Girls Triples Between Ages 12 and 15," *The Huffington Post*, accessed November 22, 2016, http://www.huffingtonpost.com/2012/07/25/depression-girls_n_1701953.html.

Mayo Clinic; "Teen Depression: Symptoms and Causes," accessed November 22, 2016.
http://www.mayoclinic.org/diseases-conditions/teen-depression/basics/causes/con-20035222.

Healthline; "Adolescent Depression," accessed November 22, 2016,
http://www.healthline.com/health/adolescent-depression#Causes2.

KidsHealth; "Depression," accessed November 22, 2016, http://kidshealth.org/parent/emotions/feelings/understanding_depression.html#.

"Teen Depression: Types of Depression," accessed November 22, 2016,
http://www.teendepression.org/info/types-of-depression/.

K. Aleisha Fetters, "8 Warning Signs of Depression You Shouldn't Ignore," accessed November 22, 2016, http://www.livestrong.com/article/91952-different-types-teenage-depression/.

"What is Cyberbullying," accessed November 22, 2016, http://www.stopbullying.gov/cyberbullying/what-is-it/.

"What is Bullying," accessed November 22, 2016, http://www.stopbullying.gov/what-is-bullying/.

Centers for Disease Control; "The Relationship Between Bullying and Suicide: What We Know and What it Means for Schools," accessed November 22, 2016, http://www.cdc.gov/violenceprevention/pdf/bullying-suicide-translation-final-a.pdf.

"Bullying and Suicide," accessed November 22, 2016, http://www.bullyingstatistics.org/content/bullying-and-suicide.html.

Megan Meier Foundation; "Bullying, Cyberbullying & Suicide Statistics," accessed November 22, 2016, http://www.meganmeierfoundation.org/statistics.html.

Mental Health America; "Self-injury (Cutting, Self-Harm or Self-Mutilation)," accessed November 22, 2016, http://www.mentalhealthamerica.net/self-injury.

"Recognizing Signs of Suicidal Tendencies," accessed November 22, 2016, http://nobullying.com/suicidal-tendencies/.

Rachelle Cassada Lohmann, "Understanding Suicide and Self-harm," *Psychology Today Online*, accessed November 22, 2016, https://www.psychologytoday.com/blog/teen-angst/201210/understanding-suicide-and-self-harm.

"Why Teens Commit Suicide," accessed November 22, 2016, http://www.teenhelp.com/teen-suicide/why-teens-commit-suicide.html.

"Cyber Bullying Statistics," accessed November 22, 2016, http://nobullying.com/cyber-bullying-statistics-2014/.

"Facts About Bullying," accessed November 22, 2016, http://www.stopbullying.gov/news/media/facts/#listing.

Bullying Statistics Online; accessed November 22, 2016, http://www.bullyingstatistics.org/.

John M. Grohol, "Common Signs of Someone Who May Be Suicidal," PsychCentral, accessed November 22, 2016, http://psychcentral.com/blog/archives/2007/10/08/common-signs-of-someone-who-may-be-suicidal/.

WebMD; "Recognizing Suicidal Behavior," accessed November 22, 2016, http://www.webmd.com/mental-health/recognizing-suicidal-behavior.

WebMD; "Recognize the Warning Signs of Suicide," accessed November 22, 2016, http://www.webmd.com/depression/guide/depression-recognizing-signs-of-suicide.

Know the Signs Online; accessed November 22, 2016, http://www.suicideispreventable.org/.

Parenting Squad; "Suicidal Tendencies: Recognize Warning Signs in Children, Young Adults," accessed November 22, 2016, http://parentingsquad.com/suicidal-tendencies-recognize-warning-signs-in-children-young-adults.

Harold Cohen, "Teenagers and Suicide," PsychCentral, accessed November 22, 2016, http://psychcentral.com/lib/teenagers-and-suicide/0001012.

"Teen Depression Statistics & Facts," accessed November 22, 2016, http://www.teenhelp.com/teen-depression/depression-statistics.html.

About Teen Depression; "Statistics—Adolescent Depression," accessed November 22, 2016, http://www.about-teen-depression.com/depression-statistics.html.

National Institutes of Health; "Major Depression Among Adolescents," accessed November 22, 2016, http://www.nimh.nih.gov/health/statistics/prevalence/major-depression-among-adolescents.shtml.

"Myths and Facts about Teen Depression," accessed November 22, 2016

The Real Guide to teenage Depression
https://www.dcsdk12.org/sites/default/files/studentwellness/Myths_and_Facts_About_Depression_and_Suicide.pdf.

National Institutes of Health; "Depression," accessed November 22, 2016, http://www.nimh.nih.gov/health/topics/depression/index.shtml.

WebMD; "Depression in Children and Teens—Prevention," accessed November 22, 2016, http://www.webmd.com/depression/tc/depression-in-childhood-and-adolescence-prevention.

Madeline Vann, "Preventing Teenage Depression," Everyday Health, accessed November 22, 2016, http://www.everydayhealth.com/depression/preventing-teenage-depression.aspx.

Beyond Blue; "How to Prevent Depression and Clinical Anxiety in Your Teenager," accessed May 2, 2017, http://www.padua.qld.edu.au/assets/Pastoral-Care/Pastoral-Care-General-Documents/3-How-to-prevent-depression-and-clinical-anxiety-in-your-teenager-part-3.pdf.

Mayo Clinic; "Teen Depression: Treatment," accessed November 22, 2016,
http://www.mayoclinic.org/diseases-conditions/teen-depression/basics/treatment/con-20035222.

WebMD; "Teen Depression: What Are the Warning Signs for Suicide?" accessed November 22, 2016,
http://www.webmd.com/depression/guide/teen-depression?page=2#3.

National Institutes of Health; "Helping Your Teen with Depression," accessed November 22, 2016,
http://www.nlm.nih.gov/medlineplus/ency/patientinstructions/000646.htm.

International Foundation for Research and Education on Depression; "Types of Depression," accessed November 22, 2016,
http://www.ifred.org/types-of-depression.

WebMD; "Types of Depression," accessed November 22, 2016,
http://www.webmd.com/depression/guide/depression-types.

Margaret L. Moline, David A. Kahn, Ruth W. Ross, Lee S. Cohen, and Lori L. Altshuler, "Premenstrual Dysphoric Disorder: A Guide for Patients and Families," accessed November 22, 2016, https://womensmentalhealth.org/wp-content/uploads/2008/04/pmdd_guide.pdf.

Beyond Blue; "Signs and Symptoms," accessed November 22, 2016, https://www.beyondblue.org.au/the-facts/depression/signs-and-symptoms.

Armon B. Neel Jr, "10 Types of Medications That Can Make You Feel Depressed," accessed November 22, 2016, http://www.aarp.org/health/drugs-supplements/info-02-2012/medications-that-can-cause-depression.html.

Ashley Yang, "Depression and Suicide and the Teenage Brain," accessed November 22, 2016, https://prezi.com/l-zhk_krzznq/depression-and-suicide-and-the-teenage-brain/.

Christopher Bergland, "Why is The Teen Brain So Vulnerable?" Psychology Today Online, https://www.psychologytoday.com/blog/the-athletes-way/201312/why-is-the-teen-brain-so-vulnerable.

Harvard Medical School; "The Adolescent Brain: Beyond Raging Hormones," accessed November 22, 2016, http://www.health.harvard.edu/mind-and-mood/the-adolescent-brain-beyond-raging-hormones.

"Substance-Induced Mood Disorder," accessed November 22, 2016,
http://www.psyweb.com/Mdisord/MoodDis/simd.jsp.

Summit Medical Group; "Substance-Induced Mood Disorder," accessed November 22, 2016,
http://www.summitmedicalgroup.com/library/adult_health/bh a_substance_induced_mood_disorder/.

Family & Youth Services Bureau; "The Hardest Adjustment: Recognizing Postpartum Depression in Teen Mothers," accessed November 22, 2016, http://ncfy.acf.hhs.gov/features/mental-health-first-step-well-being/hardest-adjustment-recognizing-postpartum-depression.

Postpartum Progress; "The Symptoms of Postpartum Depression & Anxiety (in Plain Mama English)," accessed November 22, 2016, http://www.postpartumprogress.com/the-symptoms-of-postpartum-depression-anxiety-in-plain-mama-english.

"What is Cyberbullying," accessed November 22, 2016, https://www.stopbullying.gov/cyberbullying/what-is-it/.

Maria Konnikova, "How the Internet Has Changed Bullying," The New Yorker Online, accessed November 22, 2016, http://www.newyorker.com/science/maria-konnikova/how-the-internet-has-changed-bullying.

Anne Theriault, "How to Talk to Your Teen About Depression, Suicide," *The Washington Post* Online, accessed November 22, 2016, https://www.washingtonpost.com/news/parenting/wp/2015/05/18/how-to-talk-to-your-teen-about-depression-suicide/.

Lindsay Holmes, "11 Statistics That Will Change The Way You Think About Depression," *The Huffington Post*, accessed November 22, 2016, http://www.huffingtonpost.com/2015/01/20/depression-statistics_n_6480412.html.

"20 Important Teenage Depression and Suicide Statistics," accessed November 22, 2016,

http://healthresearchfunding.org/20-important-teenage-depression-suicide-statistics/.

"Teen Depression Statistics & Facts," accessed November 22, 2016,

https://www.teenhelp.com/teen-depression/teen-depression-statistics/.

The Trevor Project; "Facts About Suicide," accessed November 22, 2016,

http://www.thetrevorproject.org/pages/facts-about-suicide.

Erlanger A. Turner, "Depression and Suicide in Black Youth," *Psychology Today* Online, accessed November 22, 2016, https://www.psychologytoday.com/blog/the-race-good-health/201507/depression-and-suicide-in-black-youth.

Science Daily; "Racial and ethnic minority adolescents less likely to receive treatment for major depression, study finds," accessed November 22, 2016,

https://www.sciencedaily.com/releases/2011/02/110222092609.htm.

Mental Health America; "Bullying and LGBT Youth," accessed November 22, 2016,

http://www.mentalhealthamerica.net/bullying-and-gay-youth.

National Alliance on Mental Illness; "LGBTQ," accessed November 22, 2016,

http://www.nami.org/Find-Support/LGBTQ.

Raising Children Network; "Low Mood and Depression: Teenagers With Autism Spectrum Disorder," accessed November 22, 2016,

http://raisingchildren.net.au/articles/autism_spectrum_disorder_mood_teenagers.html.

Center on Secondary Education for Students with ASD; "Depression in Students with ASD," accessed November 22, 2016,

http://fpg.unc.edu/sites/fpg.unc.edu/files/resources/reports-and-policy-briefs/CSESA_Depression-in-Adolescents-with-ASD.pdf.

Education Research; "Depression and Learning Disabilities," accessed November 22, 2016, http://www.ernweb.com/educational-research-articles/depression-and-learning-disabilities/.

Marie Hartwell-Walker, "Teens With Intellectual Disability Have it Harder," PsychCentral, accessed November 22, 2016, http://psychcentral.com/lib/teens-with-intellectual-disability-have-it-harder/.

Charlotte Gerber, "When Depression and Disability Go Together," VeryWell, accessed November 22, 2016, https://www.verywell.com/depression-and-disability-1094648.

Mayo Clinic; "Tween and Teen Health," accessed November 22, 2016, http://www.mayoclinic.org/healthy-lifestyle/tween-and-teen-health/in-depth/teen-depression/art-20046841?.

Leah Levy, "Classroom Strategies for Helping Depressed Teen Students," Edudemic, accessed November 22, 2016, http://www.edudemic.com/classroom-strategies-for-helping-depressed-teen-students/.

The Real Guide to teenage Depression

Lisa Firestone, "8 Ways to Actively Fight Depression" *Psychology Today* Online, accessed November 22, 2016, https://www.psychologytoday.com/blog/compassion-matters/201110/eight-ways-actively-fight-depression.

TeensHealth, "5 Ways to Help Yourself Through Depression," accessed November 22, 2016, http://kidshealth.org/en/teens/depression-tips.html.

"Coping with Depression," accessed November 22, 2016, http://www.helpguide.org/articles/depression/dealing-with-depression.htm.

Other Books by Patrice M Foster

1. Left across the Border series 1
2. Broken Teen Scars series 2
3. Tainted by Hate Series 3
4. Molding My Destiny
5. Everything I never told you: A mother's confession

Thank You

Thanks for making it through to the end of this book. We hope it was informative and able to provide you with all of the tools you need to achieve your goals whatever they may be. Join a group of parents who support and want to make a difference in teens struggling with depression.

Finally, if you found this book useful a review will be appreciated.

Printed in Great Britain
by Amazon